Illustrated

OLDSMOBILE
BUYER'S
GUIDE ™.

Motorbooks International Illustrated Buyer's Guide Series

Illustrated

OLDSMOBILE
BUYER'S GUIDE ™·

Richard M. Langworth

Motorbooks International
Publishers & Wholesalers ®

First published in 1987 by Motorbooks
International Publishers & Wholesalers Inc,
PO Box 2, 729 Prospect Avenue, Osceola
WI 54020 USA

Motorbooks International is a certified
trademark, registered with the United States
Patent Office

Printed and bound in the United States of
America

The information in this book is true and
complete to the best of our knowledge. All
recommendations are made without any
guarantee on the part of the author or
publisher, who also disclaim any liability
incurred in connection with the use of this
data or specific details

Library of Congress Cataloging-in-Publication Data
Langworth, Richard M.
    Illustrated Oldsmobile buyer's guide.

    1. Oldsmobile automobile—Purchasing. I. Title.
TL215.04L36 1987   629.2'222   87-22019.
ISBN 0-87938-270-8 (soft)

The front cover photograph is of Bob
Weggermann's beautiful Oldsmobile 4-4-2
convertible of 1970 vintage, shot by Bud Juneau

Motorbooks International books are also
available at discounts in bulk quantity for
industrial or sales-promotional use. For details
write to Special Sales Manager at the
Publisher's address

Contents

Acknowledgments

I write herein about Oldsmobiles from the past that appear significant to me, and I do so as one not without some experience of automotive history, though I vehemently deny the oft-abused title, "automotive historian."

Therefore, this book does not set out to rival the various works on Oldsmobile history. It simply selects on the basis of reasonable experience over twenty-five years the Oldsmobiles that have served as milestones in the Lansing story, and which are consequently the most important models to the collector or enthusiast.

Nor do I claim the title of Oldsmobile expert, always remembering Harry Truman's deathless aside: "An expert is a fella who doesn't want to learn anything new, because then he wouldn't be an expert anymore."

Nevertheless, the Buyer's Guides demand expertise—especially in problem areas. Here, there is no substitute for first-hand experience with the cars.

For most of the comments in the Problem Areas sections I therefore relied on the Olds club's eminent Dennis Casteele, author of the Crestline photo-documentary, *The Cars of Oldsmobile*, and his strong background and connections. Casteele, in turn, wishes to acknowledge the help of Max Hineman of DeWitt, Michigan, a veteran Olds service manager and a major vendor of New Old Stock parts, and Rod McLean, owner of McLean Brothers Garage in Lansing and a pioneer NASCAR mechanic and race car builder.

Dennis Casteele also read every word of copy and every caption to every photo (he supplied many of the latter), in an effort to save me from myself whenever I chose the wrong word or boggled the facts.

I also thank Bud Juneau for many of these photographs (including the beautiful cover car), and Barbara Harold of Motorbooks International for her usual finely tuned editing.

Finally, my thanks to Tim Parker, Britain's latest and greatest example of Reverse Lend-Lease, for his guidance, and for asking me to take on the job—which I hope you will now enjoy.

Richard M. Langworth
Hopkinton, New Hampshire
1987

Photo credits

The bulk of the factory photographs are from the collection of Dennis Casteele or the author. A number of cars were photographed by Bud Juneau especially for this book, and these are indicated in the first caption for each such car.

Introduction

A very kind reviewer in *Skinned Knuckles* said of the introduction to my first book in this series, " This is one one of the best things I've read since Henry Miller's final 'Viewpoint.' " Understandably, I immediately dug out my *Illustrated Cadillac Buyer's Guide* to reread what I wrote, and to see if it applied to Oldsmobile. Some does.

Like Cadillac, Oldsmobile was a slow starter among collector cars. But unlike Cadillac, no prewar Olds since the famous Limited has ever been considered very collectible. No Oldsmobile has ever been named a "classic" by the Classic Car Club of America (CCCA). Even the Milestone Car Society, CCCA's counterpart in the postwar era, has not named many Oldsmobiles to its roll of greats. None of which means, however, that the postwar Oldsmobiles are not collectible—quite the contrary.

Curious, when you think about it: Olds was known for years as the "experimental division" of General Motors, the place where progress happened first. Olds was first with a full-automatic transmission, the first popular-priced car with a modern ohv V-8, one of the first with a wraparound windshield and a four-door hardtop, and the first to produce a large front-wheel-drive car after World War II.

And Oldsmobile goes further back than any existing American make. This year, for example, Oldsmobile's hometown Lansing, Michigan, celebrated Olds' Ninetieth Anniversary, the first such in US automotive history. You would think all this innovation and heritage would have produced an earlier collector movement than it did.

But Oldsmobile today—or at least the postwar models I cover here—is on a roll. The Oldsmobile Club of America is one of the largest and most successful one-make clubs for US marques. Some neoclassic models like the original Rocket 88s and Fiestas are escalating rapidly in numbers. Toronado, Oldsmobile's greatest single model since the fabled Limited, has long been considered a collector piece in its early manifestations. Competition for muscle cars like the 4-4-2, Hurst/Olds and Rallye 350 is red-hot. The collectible Oldsmobile has come of age.

Perhaps the rise of certain models to blue-chip status has something to do with Oldsmobile's mixed history, which over recent years was much like Cadillac's. With the exception of the F-85 and Cutlass derivatives, Olds had long built big, heavy land yachts, which were exactly the kind that received the greatest criticism and had the most sales losses in the "dark ages" of the 1970s.

Ten or fifteen years ago, the typical Oldsmobile was expensive to buy and run, far too big, too clumsy, too *ordinary*. The contrast between cars like the Rallye 350 and the run-of-the-mill Lansing product was extreme. Perhaps subconsciously, collectors took a serious interest in the few

Oldsmobiles that *were* outstanding. If so, it made sense. Like the little girl in the nursery rhyme, when Oldsmobiles were good, they were very good indeed.

The Buyer's Guide series, which were formulated by Dean Batchelor's seminal work on Ferrari, caused a great deal of editorial mind-searching when it expanded to cover certain American makes. Batchelor could take a marque like Ferrari or Posrche and string together multichapters on every model built, because every model built was highly collectible. Not so with the typical mass-produced American makes. The variety was so much greater, and the interest level so much more variable, that a book covering *every* model might put the reader to sleep.

For Oldsmobile, therefore, instead of covering every model from 1946 to the recent past, I concentrate only on models for which a reasonable collector market already exists, or is building. That approach naturally affects the Buyer's Guide's traditional star rating system: You will find very few of these cars rated at one star, and not many two-star choices either. They are mostly three stars and above, because that is the kind of Oldsmobile I was looking for.

Investment rating

★★★★★ The Best Oldsmobiles. These are the cars you'll rarely see advertised, both because they are rather scarce, and because they usually change hands on the quiet between friends. They represent the top of the line among collectible Oldsmobiles, have the highest potential for long-term appreciation and are already very expensive. This rating will not often be applied to muscle cars, because their values have not yet exhibited the same slow but inexorable rise as the blue-chip models under this heading.

★★★★ The Next Best. Usually these are low-production models, not easily found but constantly sought after by collectors, with strong investment potential. They include all the top muscle cars, and are better short-term investments than five-star cars because more people want them *at the moment*. They are not often seen in newspaper ads but may be found fairly often in *Hemmings Motor News* and other hobby classified sections. The best source for them, however, is Olds club members—which is another reason to join the Olds club (see Appendix).

★★★ Excellent Values. These Oldsmobiles are in better supply than the first two categories (though not commonplace), and represent good investment value over the short to middle term. They are very good choices if you plan to use them for a lot of over-the-road driving. They may be "sleepers" that will move up to the higher categories later.

★★ Good Values. Like an off-year Bordeaux, these are sound, collectible cars to enjoy *right now*. All are reasonably priced (none over four figures), with good numbers to choose from, but are not moving up in value as fast as any of the first three categories. But neither are they depreciating, and haven't been for a long time.

★ Possibilities. These are the more available, often more recent models for which final collector status has not yet been settled. Or they are cars that have long been on the scene without moving up much in value. But all are definitely collectible, which is a minimum for inclusion here.

*　　*　　*

As in all things, the car collector must rely on common sense. The top-of-the-line 1953 convertible, of which fewer than 500 were built, is a stratosphere-priced, five-star collector Oldsmobile, while the top-of-the-line 1954 convertible is *anything but*. The difference? The '53 was an entirely unique car, with its own body and novel Motorama features such as a metal convertible top cover and a then-unique wraparound windshield.

Convertibles and, to a lesser extent, hardtops (particularly the two-door kind) are inevitably better investments than closed cars, but they are also more difficult to restore. For example, the '53 Fiesta is more difficult than the '54 Starfire. If you have a choice, buy the best one available. It will be less expensive in the long run.

New cars built since about 1968 are rated more by their estimated *potential* value. In one case (see Chapter 28), they may still actually be depreciating in value. Once again, open models are preferable to closed, deluxe versions to standard. Unique trim packages or low-volume, interesting models are good bets for future collectibility.

Seasoned collectors will find this superfluous, but it ought to be mentioned for the record: "Old" Oldsmobiles not discussed in this book are those which, in my opinion, have little or no collector followings. These tend to be low-line models, or high-volume body styles like four-door sedans. Of course there are exceptions: A stripped 88 two-door sedan from the mid-fifties, which ordinarily would not be collectible, might interest a collector if it had 500 miles on its odometer. A plug-ordinary '63 F-85 coupe might be of personal interest to a collector who learned to drive on the same model—but to no one else. But, despite the opinions of countless owners of well-worn old cars, age alone does not bestow a car with any special status.

A word about prices

The lack of long lists of values for cars herein is not an omission. I simply don't believe in them.

The fact is, collector cars are not bought and sold regularly enough or in such numbers for there to be a genuine guide to their values. The National Automobile Dealer's Association *Used Car Guide* is just for everyday used cars.

And the collector market is volatile. Curiously, it seems to rise and fall in inverse proportion to the state of the economy. Times are good right now, but the market is sluggish. Six years ago when times were bad, the collector car market was flying high. I am not sure what this means, but some economists say it is the result of people looking for tangibles to hang onto when the value of money seems to be dropping out of sight.

Where rough ideas of price ranges (like "five figures") seem worth mentioning, they are. For model-by-model, body-by-body lists of prices, down to the last dollar, please look elsewhere. But for heaven's sake, don't expect the *actual* prices to have much relation to those listed prices.

It seems to a lot of people in the old-car appraisal field that the prices generally found in *Hemmings* and similar sources are much higher than in reality. Out of curiosity, a colleague with a WATS line dialed one hundred *Hemmings* advertisers a month after their ads ran to ask if they'd sold their cars. Five percent had.

Rich Taylor, author of the entertaining book, *Modern Classics,* once compared buying a collector car to "dickering for slaves in old Algiers," or something like that. There was a grain of truth in it.

Chapter 1

Custom Cruiser 98 convertible

★★★★

1946-47

HISTORY

Top of the line for Oldsmobile in the first two postwar years, this luxurious convertible rode the longest wheelbase of the postwar era. Priced up to $442 over the next 98, it competed (embarrassingly) head-on with the Buick Roadmaster convertible and (more comfortably) with the Chrysler New Yorker. Obviously a prewar car, it offered high quality but low performance.

The 98 lacked the stylish glamour of the competitive Buick Roadmaster convertible, and was usually sold new with blackwall tires in 1946, though restorers have generally shod them with wide whites. The all-chrome hood ornament is one way to tell the 1946 model from the '47.

IDENTIFICATION

1946: All-chrome hood ornament, small Oldsmobile nameplate on thick fender brightwork.

1947: Plastic fins on hood ornament and longer nameplate on fender molding which tapered more to the rear.

PERFORMANCE AND UTILITY

A big, heavy cruiser, happiest on the highway, where it will maintain modern speeds if you keep your foot off. All the pros and cons of the typical early-forties design: doors, hood and deck clang shut like manhole covers, multitube radios emit a "fat" sound not duplicated by the best modern transistors. A real handful on any kind of challenging road, and thirsty. No performance to speak of, especially with Hydramatic, which ninety-eight percent of them had.

PROBLEM AREAS

Not relatively susceptible to rust and corrosion, but the prospective purchase should nevertheless be checked in all the usual places: rocker panels, wheel arches, floors and the areas between body seams. The smaller L-head engine was no powerhouse, but is known for its longevity. High-mileage examples should be given a valve job and decarbonization as a matter of routine, however.

A nonbaffled oil pan could add to lubricant distribution problems. These cars may experience starting problems, particularly in wet conditions or if the engine is out of tune.

SUMMARY AND PROSPECTS

In a mediocre period for any make, wise collectors select the top of the line and the lowest production model, preferably an open body style. The Custom Cruiser 98

Another view of the '46, showing the pontoon fender styling of Harley Earl, which carried on through the front doors—very radical when Harley came up with it but old-hat after the war when the emphasis was soon on fenderless body sides. Convertible tops were black with a small oblong backlight.

is all three—far more desirable than the stubby 60-series convertibles on their much shorter wheelbases. Fine original or well-restored 98 convertibles have topped $20,000 in auctions, but they rarely appear owing to very low production. In the absence of a 98 convertible, the 98 coupe (but not the sedan) may be a better buy than a smaller open car from the same period (1946-47 66, 1947 68). Convertibles will continue to slowly appreciate.

PRODUCTION	*1946*	*1947*
convertible coupe	874	3,940

1946-47 Custom Cruiser 98

ENGINE

Type	8-cyl in-line L-head, water-cooled, cast-iron block and heads
Bore x stroke	3.25x3.88 in.
Displacement	257.1 ci
Valve operation	side-valve
Compression ratio	6.5:1
Carburetion	dual-throat downdraft
Bhp	110 gross at 3600 rpm

CHASSIS & DRIVETRAIN

Transmission	3-spd, Hydra-matic opt
Rear axle ratio	3.63:1
Front suspension	independent, coil springs, tube shocks
Rear suspension	live axle, coil springs, tube shocks

GENERAL

Wheelbase	127 in.
Overall length	216 in.
Track	58 in. front, 62 in. rear
Tire size	7.00x15
Weight	4,025-4,075 lb

PERFORMANCE

Acceleration	0-60: 25 sec
Top speed	88 mph
Fuel mileage	13-16 mpg

While the tire industry was bereft of whitewalls, dealers often added "donut" rings to simulate them, but they weren't visually effective. Note the longer nameplate on the front fender and (difficult to see in this photo) the part-plastic hood ornament, which are the two main exterior identifying features of the 1974 model.

With its top down, the 1947 98 was an impressive cruiser, and it certainly looks better in light colors. Whitewalls continued in short supply, and the restorer interested in invoking the feel of the era might save some money by using blackwalls, which look all right on this model.

Wood-bodied station wagon

1946-49

★★★

HISTORY

Oldsmobile was swift to build wagons, slow to capitalize on them. It had a woody in its line as early as 1935, and a production version of its own manufacture by 1940, but sales of those clumsy, utilitarian models were slow, and mainly to hotels and livery services. The last woodies—by then the lumber was limited to tailgates and beltlines—were sold in early 1949. Through 1948, wood bodies were supplied to Oldsmobile by Hercules; the handful of 1949 woodies had Fisher bodies.

IDENTIFICATION

1946: All-chromed hood ornament, narrow Oldsmobile nameplate on thick fender molding.

1947: Plastic fins on hood ornament, wider nameplate on fender molding, which tapered to the rear.

1948: Stylized aero hood ornament with stubby plastic fins, round hood badge instead of the previous shield, full-length lower body bright molding.

1949: All-new styling with two- instead of four-bar grille, ringed-world hood em-

The only illustration I could find of the 1947 woody, showing new 68 model (production was a scant 492) with otherwise-unchanged Hercules body. It sold for about $2,200 base price, the highest for any 1947 model. Birch and mahogany woodwork is the chief restoration problem on all these cars.

blem, Futuramic badge on front of lower body molding.

PERFORMANCE AND UTILITY

These wagons vary widely in performance, depending on the model: Six-cylinder types are severely underpowered, weighing 4,000-plus pounds with two or more passengers. Flathead eights (through 1948) are hardly better, while Rocket V-8 88s are relatively sprightly. Hydra-matic limits performance of all models, but was standard only on 88s.

Utility is superb—seven feet of cargo area with the middle and rear seats out, eight-passenger capacity with all the seats in. Ideal for the hard-bitten swap-meet prowler.

PROBLEM AREAS

On all woodies, the first area of trouble is the wood. It is also the second and third areas. Examples range from the unrestorable to the decent but, ironically, even well-

A nice period photo: the 1946 Olds woody wagon in a hall bedecked with the flags of the World War II Allies. The wood body was built by Hercules of Ionia, Michigan, through the end of 1947. Note the fabric roof, difficult to maintain and prone to leaks.

maintained cars may suffer from varnish buildup in the crevices or dry rot working its way up from underneath. Before purchasing, one should consider the amount of work the wood will require, one's ability to do it and the cost. (For mechanical comments, see Chapter 1 for flatheads and Chapter 3 for V-8s.)

Some small interior trim items exclusive to wagons—particularly seat and tailgate hardware—are difficult to find. Troublesome to replace and prone to deterioration is the "parchment" type headliner found in several years of the Olds woodies.

SUMMARY AND PROSPECTS

Once the ugly ducklings of Detroit, woody wagons are prized today for their superb carpentry and fine materials (white ash and mahogany in Olds' case). Fine ex-amples have long sold for five figures, and $15,000 would not be too much to pay for the ninety-point showstopper.

PRODUCTION	1946	1947	1948	1949
66	140	968	840	—
66 Deluxe	—	—	553	—
68	—	492	760	—
68 Deluxe	—	—	554	—
76	—	—	—	—
76 Deluxe	—	—	—	1,545*
88	—	—	—	—
88 Deluxe	—	—	—	1,355*

* These figures include steel-bodied wagons which in effect replaced the woodies in early 1949. Separate breakdowns are not available, but I'd guess that woodies numbered about a third of these totals. (See also Chapter 5.)

The 1948 facelift: a new hood ornament, the Oldsmobile name shifted from front fenders to hood, a round hood badge and matching hubcaps. This is a black 66; other wagon colors were Ambassador red. Tawnee buff and Ivy green. The setting is the Lansing, Michigan, railroad station. Note the brightmetal splash guard, new in '48.

An interesting photo, labeled a '48 model by the factory, but carrying the 1947 hood and fender badges and hood ornament (despite '48 hubcaps). This was either a prototype or early production model using up leftover '47 trim. Compare with the preceding photo: Both cars carry the cadet sun visor, now rarely seen, a $30.25 dealer accessory.

From the rear three-quarter view, note the beautiful carpentry of the wooden wagon body, which was Fisher-built this year.

M 25·44

Quality-built throughout, the wagon was upholstered in tan leatherette and the cargo bay was carpeted with metal runners. Tailgate folded flat and lights flopped down to the vertical if the car was to be driven with the tail open. A Lucite lens is mounted on the dash to "see" traffic lights despite the cadet sun visor.

1946-49 Wood-bodied wagon (6-cyl)

ENGINE

Type	6-cyl in-line L-head, water-cooled, cast-iron block and heads
Bore x stroke	3.50x4.13 in.
Displacement	238.1 ci
Valve operation	side-valve
Compression ratio	6.5:1
Carburetion	2-bbl downdraft
Bhp	100 gross at 3600 rpm

CHASSIS & DRIVETRAIN

Transmission	3-spd, Hydra-matic opt (std on 88)
Rear axle ratio	3.90:1
Front suspension	independent, coil springs, tube shocks
Rear suspension	live axle, coil springs, tube shocks

GENERAL

Wheelbase	119 in., 119.5 in. (1949)
Overall length	205 in., 205.7 in. (1949)
Track	58.0 in. front, 62.0 in. rear
Tire size	6.00x16 (1946-47), 6.50x15 (1948), 7.10x15 (1949)
Weight	3,445-3,520 lb

PERFORMANCE

Acceleration	0-60: 30 sec
Top speed	83 mph
Fuel mileage	13-18 mpg

Note: for 68, see Chapter 1; for 88, see Chapter 3

There wasn't much wood left by 1949, but it beautifully complemented the new Futuramic styling. With minimal woodwork steel tops, these are the easiest woodies to restore or maintain, and they are also clearly the best looking.

As before, the tailgates were designed to create minimal obstruction and the taillamps folded down, one also illuminated the license plate.

Woodies were discontinued in early 1949 in favor of steel-bodied wagons which simulated the wood look.

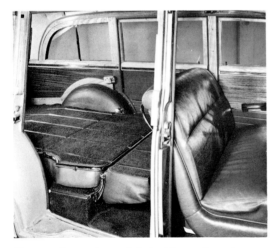

Plenty of wood was left inside, and workmanship continued on a high level. The plethora of wood or decal surfaces and brightmetal means that an interior restoration may not be cheap; on the other hand, the leatherette upholstery was impervious to wear and is usually found in good condition.

Chapter 3

Futuramic 98

1948-49

★★★★	convertible
★★★	club and town sedan
★★	4-door sedan

HISTORY

Along with Cadillac, Oldsmobile trumped the Ford and Chrysler opposition as well as three of its sister divisions by introducing its first all-new postwar redesign in 1948. Unlike Cadillac, the new styling was not line-wide, but confined to the upper-priced 98s—and not introduced until the remaining old designs had been sold off.

The overall direction was given by Harley Earl, the detail execution for Oldsmobile by Art Ross. The styling inspiration was the beautiful Lockheed P-38 fighter aircraft, whose propeller housing Ross duplicated

Today, one of the most desirable postwar Oldsmobiles, the Futuramic 98 for 1948, introduced Lansing's first postwar restyle, but its engine remained the inline eight with 115 hp. The push-button hydraulic system governing the top was extended, on convertibles, to power the seats and windows as well.

in the 1949 headlamp/air scoop/parking lamp ensembles.

Like the '48 Cadillacs, these Oldsmobiles were magnificent designs. Among closed cars the club sedan was outstanding, while the Town sedan (fastback), unpopular then, is also interesting. Both these fastbacks deserve more collector attention.

In 1949 came the new Rocket V-8 engine (and another new body style, the Holiday hardtop, detailed in Chapter 4).

IDENTIFICATION

1948: Separate headlamp and parking lamps, round hood badge over separate block-letter "Oldsmobile."

1949: Headlamp/air scoop/parking lamp combination, ringed-world hood badge, Futuramic name on front of lower body molding, push-button door handles and rear-fender chrome moldings housing tail-lamps over stop lamps.

PERFORMANCE AND UTILITY

Naturally, performance was instantly transformed in 1949 by the potent new 303.7 ci Rocket V-8 with its 135 bhp. Though 100-odd pounds lighter than the earlier 98, this was still a lot of automobile even for the new engine, which did better in the lighter 88s.

The four-door sedan version of the Futuramic 98 came in standard and deluxe trim, the latter indicated by the suffix "D" on the model number. About six out of seven 98 sedans were deluxe versions, though this one is a standard. The differences were inside.

Olds' previous standards of luxury prevailed in the deluxe closed models (which carried a D model number), fitted with broadcloth upholstery, clock, deluxe steering wheel and floor mats, chrome wheel trim rings, 8.20×15 tires and fold-down rear center armrests. DX model numbers signified hydraulic window-lift Deluxes; hydraulics were standard in convertibles.

PROBLEM AREAS

Not rust-prone, but water leaks are common. Exclusive-to-1948 parts sometimes hard to find. Hydraulic systems and convertible tops are troublesome. The V-8 may have starting problems when hot (alleviated when 12-volts came along a few years later). Warm-weather vapor lock and noisy valve lifters are easily cured problems. Rear axles and front spindles suffered from V-8 wallop and should be checked often.

Since Futuramics were an entirely new body style, there were some teething problems during assembly, as well as resultant fit and finish lapses, which may require correction by fastidious restorers.

SUMMARY AND PROSPECTS

An overlooked group of Oldsmobiles owing to the popularity and importance of the smaller 88 (1949-on), the Futuramic 98 was historically significant and handsome to look at—and check some of the low production figures.

The scarce club and Town sedans are underpriced on today's depressed market. Selling prices have not extended much beyond $12,000 for any, yet all models will move up, especially the '49s with their V-8 engines and upgraded trim.

PRODUCTION	1948	1949
club sedan	2,311	3,849
Deluxe club sedan	11,949	16,200
4-door sedan	5,605	8,820
Deluxe 4-door sedan	32,456	49,001
convertible coupe	12,914	12,602
Town sedan (fastback)	—	2,859
Deluxe Town sedan	—	2,974

The 1949 Futuramic 98 convertible with its powerful new 135 hp Rocket V-8 and enhanced styling was altogether a more desirable car than its '48 counterpart. Design features included the first ringed-world emblems on fenders and hood, and air scoops under headlamps similar to the classic Lockheed P-38 fighter aircraft.

The 98 sedan for 1949, which remained Oldsmobile's best-selling model again this year. Note the two-tone pattern, which extended down through the roof posts to the beltline, unlike certain other GM cars which had duotones only in the roof area.

1948-49 Futuramic 98

ENGINE

Type ... 8-cyl 90-deg V-type, water-cooled, cast-iron block and heads
Bore x stroke .... 3.75x3.44 in.
Displacement .... 303.7 ci
Valve operation .... overhead
Compression ratio 7.25:1
Carburetion .... 2-bbl downdraft
Bhp .... 135 gross at 3600 rpm

CHASSIS & DRIVETRAIN

Transmission .... 3-spd (std 1948), Hydra-matic (std 1949)
Rear axle ratio .... 3.73:1 (std 1948), 3.56:1 (std 1949)
Front suspension ...... independent, coil springs, tube shocks
Rear suspension .... live axle, coil springs, tube shocks

GENERAL

Wheelbase .... 125 in.
Overall length .... 213.5 in. (1948), 210.0 in. (1949)
Track .... 57 in. front, 59 in. rear
Tire size 7.00x15 (1948), 7.60x15 (1949)
Weight .... 3,880 lb (1948), 3,820 lb (1949)

PERFORMANCE

Acceleration .... 0-60: 13 sec (1949)
Top speed .... 88 mph (1948), 96 mph (1949)
Fuel mileage .... 13-16 mpg (1948), 14-17 mpg (1949)
Note: For 1949; for 1948 hp 115; also, see Chapter 1

Chapter 4

Futuramic 98 Holiday hardtop

★★★★★

1949

HISTORY

While a five-star rating is going some, it really *is* deserved in the case of this historically important yet rarely seen Oldsmobile. Along with the Buick Riviera and Cadillac Coupe de Ville, the 98 Holiday shares the title of the original "hardtop convertible."

All three were the deft creations of GM's Art and Color Studio under Harley Earl, designed to combine the luxury interior and airiness of a convertible with the solidity of a closed car.

Buick built over 4,300 Rivieras; Cadillac built only 2,150 Coupe de Villes, but a huge

The rarest, most desirable and historically significant 1949 98 was the new Holiday hardtop. Few were built because of its late introduction, but the survivors are highly sought after today.

Most were two-toned as is this model. Chrome highlights over the rear fenders were another aspect of the 1949 facelift on all Futuramics.

proportion seem to have survived. I know of only two Oldsmobile 98 Holidays, but the Oldsmobile Club knows of a few more. Many critics of design consider the Olds version of the hardtop the nicest.

IDENTIFICATION

The only Oldsmobile hardtop with a divided windshield.

PERFORMANCE AND UTILITY

Since all of them came with the Rocket V-8, off-the-line performance is good and high-speed cruising excellent, thanks to a cushy suspension carrying nearly two tons of curb weight. Nearly all are found with Hydra-matic.

Virtues of the hardtop style are the same now as they were then: an open-air feel with no danger to your blown-dry haircut, and no heavy-duty maintenance problems for the roof. A super-looking luxury car of high quality.

PROBLEM AREAS

Some fit problems occurred with the new Holiday body style. All special Holiday trim is rare and doesn't interchange with later Holidays. Vinyl should not be substituted on leather-upholstered models. (See Chapter 3 for engine/chassis tips.)

SUMMARY AND PROSPECTS

Most price guides show 98 convertibles from this model-year some four times as expensive as the Holiday. I suspect they have not taken into account the Holiday's scarcity (there were four ragtops built to every hardtop) and historic importance. Future years will see quantum leaps in this model's value, and if you can find one for under $10,000 right now, it's a steal.

PRODUCTION
3,006

1949 Futuramic 98 Holiday

ENGINE

Type	8-cyl 90-deg V-type, water-cooled, cast-iron block and heads
Bore x stroke	3.75x3.44 in.
Displacement	303.7 ci
Valve operation	overhead
Compression ratio	7.25:1
Carburetion	2-bbl downdraft
Bhp	135 gross at 3600 rpm

CHASSIS & DRIVETRAIN

Transmission	Hydra-matic
Rear axle ratio	3.56:1
Front suspension	independent, coil springs, tube shocks
Rear suspension	live axle, coil springs, tube shocks

GENERAL

Wheelbase	125 in.
Overall length	210 in.
Track	57 in. front, 59 in. rear
Tire size	7.60x15
Weight	4,000 lb

PERFORMANCE

Acceleration	0-60: 13 sec
Top speed	96 mph
Fuel mileage	13-17 mpg

Chapter 5

Steel-bodied station wagon

1949-50

★★

HISTORY

Traditionally the experimental division of General Motors, Olds was often first-out with new ideas, and the all-steel wagon is among these. Here, however, Oldsmobile was not quite alone: Chevy, Pontiac and Plymouth introduced similar models the same year, and if you count Willys, there had been a steel Jeep wagon since 1946.

Of all these, the Olds was the most expensive, and that is perhaps why it didn't sell. Thus Oldsmobile opted out of the wagon business in 1950, missing the wagon craze of the mid-fifties. It wasn't until 1957 that Olds re-entered the field with the Fiesta.

IDENTIFICATION

1949: Futuramic styling with ringed-world hood badge, Futuramic nameplate on leading edge of lower body molding.

1950: Plain lower body molding with no nameplate.

Replacement for the woody was the all-steel 1949 Oldsmobile wagon which arrived early in the year. It used woodgrained steel to simulate the former wood components, although some wood remained to decorate the interior. Compare the chrome beltline molding, which ends far to the rear, with the truncated style of the 1950 model.

PERFORMANCE AND UTILITY

Like the woody wagon that shared the 1949 line, the all-steel version offered huge cargo space (eighty square feet) with the center and rear seats out, and eight-passenger capacity with them in. The 88 wagon was a spirited performer with the new V-8 (see Chapter 6), while the six, though a fine engine, had a heavy job.

PROBLEM AREAS

Few body parts interchange with woodies; the woody parchment headliner problem still exists (see Chapter 2). Decals and exclusive trim pieces are hard to find. Mechanical interchangeability is good. (See Chapter 3 for engine/chassis notes.)

SUMMARY AND PROSPECTS

While not a high roller among collectible Oldsmobiles, the all-steel wagons should be considered historically important—indeed the most luxurious of their type that could be bought in 1949-50. Deluxe trim versions (model number D) are actually more common than standards, but it makes little difference. Not destined to achieve high value, they're a good buy today, and certainly something different—if you can find one.

PRODUCTION	1949	1950
76	—	121
76 Deluxe	1,545*	247
88	—	1,830
88 Deluxe	1,355*	552

These figures include wood-bodied wagons, probably about a third of the total.

1949-50 steel-bodied station wagon

ENGINE
Type ... 8-cyl 90-deg V-type, water-cooled, cast-iron block and heads
Bore x stroke . . . . 3.75x3.44 in.
Displacement . . . . 303.7 ci
Valve operation . . . . overhead
Compression ratio 7.25:1
Carburetion . . . . 2-bbl downdraft
Bhp . . . . 135 gross at 3600 rpm

CHASSIS & DRIVETRAIN
Transmission . . . . 3-spd (std 76), Hydra-matic (88)
Rear axle ratio 3.90:1 (76), 3.73:1 (88)
Front suspension . . . . . . independent, coil springs, tube shocks
Rear suspension . . . . live axle, coil springs, tube shocks

GENERAL
Wheelbase . . . . 119.5 in.
Overall length . . . . 207 in.
Track . . . . 57 in. front, 59 in. rear
Tire size 7.10x15 (76), 7.60x15 (88)
Weight . . . . 3,680-3,780 lb

PERFORMANCE
Acceleration . . . . 0-60: 13 sec (88)
Top speed . . . . 85 mph (76), 96 mph (88)
Fuel mileage . . . . 15-19 mpg

This and all following photos in this chapter are of a 1950 88 steel wagon owned by California dealer Avery Greene. Photography by Bud Juneau.

The 1950 wagons would be Oldsmobile's last until 1957—in 1950, there just didn't seem to be much of a market for them. However, the '50 model was subtly changed and improved from the '49 in various ways.

The tailgate and rear window button up smoothly, and the ringed-world emblem means there is no mistaking this for another brand from the rear. Visibility was also improved from the woody wagons through a slightly larger glass area. Restoration of the woodgraining may prove a problem.

The taillamps swing down automatically as you lower the tailgate, as opposed to earlier models, where you had to flop them down by hand.

A compartment under the rear seat houses the jack and tools.

The spare tire is housed out of the way in a floor compartment, unlike many contemporary wagons which bolted it upright to the rear inner wall, or even to the inside of a rear door!

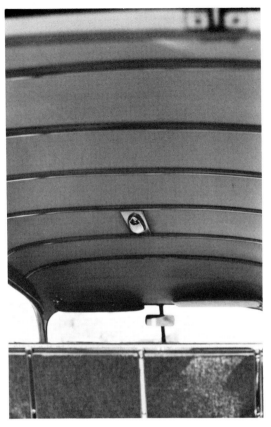

Unlike the '49 wagon, the chrome strip ends at the wing vents on the 1950 models. Replacing the door sections, if either is missing, could be a long and difficult process; it is probably worth taking a chance on repairing and replating this odd piece of pot metal.

"Parchment" headliner, a problem for restorers, is in exceptional condition on Avery Greene's car. Wood trim strips are a nice touch, similar to the dummy top bows in GM hardtops.

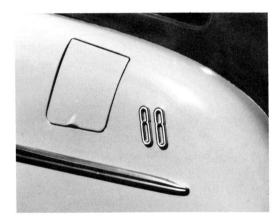

There is no mistaking the wagon model in 1950, as there was in previous years. Greene's 88 clearly identifies itself on the rear fenders.

Door moldings are beautifully wood-grained, but bad ones will present the restorer with problems.

A new, more elaborate rocket hood ornament was a feature of all the 1950 models, but is a fairly difficult item to find at swap meets.

Asymmetric in design for the first time in 1949, the Olds dashboard was little changed. Greene's car is equipped with the central clock and radio, Hydra-matic and fresh-air heater.

Smooth and sleek, the '50 88 is my personal favorite among Olds wagons. It was built with unyielding integrity, and had the room and power to handle most everything asked of it.

Chapter 6

88
1949-51

★★★★

HISTORY

The first high-performance Oldsmobile in history, National Association of Stock Car Auto Racing (NASCAR) champion in those years, which also happen to have been a period of superb styling. While the 88, with Olds' new high-compression V-8 in the lighter body, legitimately ranks as the first muscle car, the combination came together with no thought of racing.

General Manager Sherrod Skinner had decided to concentrate strictly on V-8 engines, and wanted the six-cylinder plant for other purposes. Hot-rodders and racing teams did the rest.

Oldsmobile won five out of eight Grand Nationals in 1949, ten out of nineteen in 1950 and twenty out of forty-one in 1951. 88s remained contenders in 1952-1955, though the NASCAR title was then held by the Hudson Hornet. By '51 they were the bottom-line models.

IDENTIFICATION

1949: Two-bar grille, "Oldsmobile" in block letters above grille, chrome taillight bracket extended to crown of rear fender.

1950: Chrome molding from headlight through front door, "88" with rocket on trunk lid, one-piece windshield on later models.

1951: Chrome strip along bottom of body, name in block letters around crest attached to chrome bar on hood.

PERFORMANCE AND UTILITY

Nimble and fast, the typical Hydra-matic 88 would run 0-60 in about twelve seconds and a 19.5 second quarter mile, with a top speed of 93-96 mph. A '50 model was the fastest car *Motor Trend* had tested up to that time. Yet fuel mileage was good, at least

The Rocket V-8 was the first of its kind in a popular-priced car, and it was destined to turn Oldsmobile's image around. With the Cadillac, Chrysler and Studebaker V-8s of the same period, it led the industry into the age of unbridled horsepower. But early Rockets present certain problems to the collector.

16 mpg; a '50 88 averaged 20.19 mpg from Los Angeles to the Grand Canyon. Big, roomy bodies on the all-coil suspension made for space and comfort as well as speed.

PROBLEM AREAS

Rocket V-8s were often run hard, especially by second and third owners, and the 88's early Hydra-matic had a limited tolerance for abuse. Stick models (rare) had a tougher Cadillac gearbox. Water leaks may occur. Competition is tough for NOS or even good used parts, trim especially. Not prone to rust, but *do* look for it.

SUMMARY AND PROSPECTS

Named early to the select list of "Milestones" by The Milestone Car Society, the 88 has long been one of the most highly collectible Oldsmobiles.

While NASCAR people obviously raced closed cars, Holiday hardtops and convertibles are the most desirable. Prices for fine examples are well into five figures now. With historical importance, good looks, quality and performance to recommend them, these first Rocket 88s will continue to appreciate quickly.

Look for Deluxe models with more elaborate trim, rear robe rail, ashtrays and so on.

Another unusual 1950 item—a fender crown *without* the back-up light. Bud Juneau photo.

Best model of the first year, the 1949 convertible was a smoothly styled road car. Examples are rare today, and collectors are willing to expend major capital to restore them.

PRODUCTION	1949	1950	1951
club sedan	16,887	14,705	—
Deluxe club sedan	11,820	16,388	—
club coupe	6,562	10,684	—
Deluxe club coupe	4,999	10,772	—
convertible	5,434	9,127	—
Town sedan	2,859	—	—
Deluxe Town sedan	2,974	—	—
sedan	23,342	40,301	22,848
Deluxe sedan	23,044	100,810	—
wagon	—	1,830	—
Deluxe wagon	1,355	552	—
2-door sedan	—	23,889	11,792
Deluxe 2-door sedan	—	26,672	—
Holiday hardtop	—	1,366	—
Deluxe Holiday hardtop	—	11,316	—

1949-51 88

ENGINE

Type ..... 8-cyl 90-deg V-8, water-cooled, cast-iron block and heads

Bore x stroke . . . . 3.75x3.44 in.

Displacement . . . . 303.7 ci

Valve operation . . . . hydraulic

Compression ratio 7.25:1, 7.5:1 (1951)

Carburetion . . . . 2-bbl downdraft

Bhp . . . . 135 gross at 3600 rpm

CHASSIS & DRIVETRAIN

Transmission . . . . 3-spd, Hydra-matic opt

Rear axle ratio 3.73:1, 3.64:1 (1951)

Front suspension . . . . . . independent, coil springs, tube shocks

Rear suspension . . . . live axle, coil springs, tube shocks

GENERAL

Wheelbase . . . . 119.5 in.

Overall length . . . . 207 in., 204 in. (1951)

Track . . . . 57 in. front, 59 in. rear

Tire size 7.60x15

Weight . . . . 3,435-3,945 lb

PERFORMANCE

Acceleration . . . . 0-60: 13 sec

Top speed . . . . 95-100 mph

Fuel mileage . . . . 16-20 mpg

A 1950 88 Holiday owned by Bob Brelsford, with the more typical light-over-dark two-tone color combination. Bud Juneau photo.

The typical 1950 Oldsmobile dash, with clock, radio and Hydra-matic. Bud Juneau photo.

Bud Juneau's 1950 88 convertible with the dealer display hood, which used a section of clear plexiglass to allow the hot Rocket V-8 to be seen by sales prospects. The clear hood is a valuable but scarce item to look for. It is weatherproof and practical to use on the road.

This dash from a convertible owned by Dave Rymal is unusual because of the standard shift, ringless (non-deluxe) wheel, and the absence of both clock and radio. Bud Juneau photo.

Club coupe versions of the 1948 88 are rare today—only about 11,500 were built in both standard and Deluxe guise. The foreshortened superstructure of club coupe gives them an edge against most other cars among collectors, and this is definitely a body style to look for when it comes to Rocket 88s.

The most common of the 88s are the four-door sedans; this is a 1950 model. Four-doors are the least expensive and easiest to find today, but they lack the sporty panache of the ragtops and Holidays or the clean good looks of the coupes and fastbacks, so they are not widely sought after.

Oldsmobile began going to one-piece wind-shields in 1950, but not on all models. The six-cylinder 76 (left) retained the divided wind-shield, the 88 Holiday (right) did not—although a few early '50 88s did have the two-piece version. Bud Juneau photo.

The Holiday hardtop made its debut as an 88 model in 1950, and this car belongs to Olds Division. Its two-tone paint job of light yellow and black is a typical and attractive pattern of the day. The Lockheed P-38 aircraft was an obvious styling influence.

Chapter 7

Super 88
1951

HISTORY

In 1951, Oldsmobile Division instituted vast model rationalization and winnowed-out the slow-selling versions as well as all six-cylinder 76 models. This left a baseline two- and four-door 88 (see Chapter 6), and a deluxe line of five 88s now called Supers, on a one-half-inch-longer wheelbase. These were the most luxurious and elaborate 88s to date.

A factory photograph of the 1951 Super 88 convertible. The most expensive 88, it sold for $2,673 base price and close to $3,000 as typically equipped. Styling was getting heavier, and the '51 generally isn't as highly collectible as the 1949-50 versions.

IDENTIFICATION

Grille formed by one chrome bar curved down at both ends and one straight horizontal bar that extended past the bumper guards. Vertical chrome molding above gravel deflectors on rear fenders, and a three-piece back-up light were other distinguishing characteristics.

PERFORMANCE AND UTILITY

Same as 88s; see Chapter 6.

The 1951 Oldsmobile hood ornament was only slightly modified.

Evolution of the sub-headlamp scoop for 1951, with small vertical blades surmounting the parking lamp—an easy way to tell this year's model.

This 1951 Super 88 Deluxe Holiday hardtop, owned by Don Baldwin, is equipped with the optional external visor and spotlamp. This and the following detail photographs of the same car are by Bud Juneau.

The unchanged V-8 suffers from valve-lifter noise and hard starting. Accessibility remained very good in these 88s of the early 1950s, however, so working on it isn't a trial of dexterity.

PROBLEM AREAS

Same as 1949-51 88 models (see Chapter 6), with the added problem of difficult-to-find body trim and interior parts unique to the Super. Some trim-fitting problems, since it was a first-year model. Plastic trim, chrome and fabrics scarce. Chrome quality was not good. V-8 still hard to start and was prone to lifter noise.

SUMMARY AND PROSPECTS

The only hardtop and convertible 88s this year were Supers, and open models are always collectible. But enthusiast interest lies more in 1949-50 models, so '51s are only moderately good collectibles.

PRODUCTION	1951
club coupe	7,328
4-door sedan	90,131
2-door sedan	34,963
convertible	3,854
Holiday hardtop	14,180

1951 Super 88	
ENGINE	
As per 1949-51 88.	
CHASSIS & DRIVETRAIN	
As per 1949-51 88.	
GENERAL	
Wheelbase	120 in.
Overall length	204 in.
Track	57 in. front, 59 in. rear
Tire size	7.60x15
Weight	3,557-3,831 lb
PERFORMANCE	
As per 1949-51 88.	

Another way to tell a '51 at a glance, the name shifted from below the ringed-world emblem to above, where it curved around the top. Globes in pristine condition are difficult to come by.

Chapter 8

Fiesta
1953

★★★★★

HISTORY

A special limited-edition luxury convertible based on the standard 98 bodyshell, one of three GM show cars for the public introduced that year (Buick Skylark and Cadillac Eldorado were the others). Predictive styling, with wraparound windshield, spinner hubcaps (beloved by customizers, and widely copied) and flush-folding soft top.

The Fiesta cost a lot and sold slowly, but one couldn't fault the spec. It came with a specially tuned version of the Rocket V-8, a custom, leather-upholstered interior and just about every option as standard: Hydramatic, power steering, power brakes, electric windows, power seats, Autronic-eye automatic headlamp dimming, whitewalls, radio/heater and more.

More a glamour item than a serious marketing foray, the Fiesta was withdrawn almost as suddenly as it appeared. Buick likewise dropped the Riviera after 1954. Obviously such ultra-cars were best sold by

This factory photograph of the Fiesta shows its rakishly low beltline and predictive wraparound windshield, features shared by the Buick Skylark and Cadillac Eldorado in 1953. The spinner wheel covers soon became an Olds tradition, and were beloved by the custom car crowd in the fifties.

Cadillac, whose Eldorado stayed in production and enjoyed increasing sales in later years.

IDENTIFICATION

Oldsmobile's only wraparound windshield on a 1953 model. Unique metal soft top boot; distinctive center chrome strip on trunk lid and "Fiesta" script above keyhole.

PERFORMANCE AND UTILITY

Despite a 5 bhp advantage from its special tuning, the Fiesta V-8 was handicapped by weight: 4,453 pounds at the curb, about 350 more than the standard 98 convertible. Cushy suspension settings make for no alacrity on twisty roads. Not nearly as exciting as the 88 to drive, but that wasn't its prime purpose.

PROBLEM AREAS

Virtually impossible to find now, surviving Fiestas are highly prized and hardly ever advertised in the old-car classifieds. You get one by making a lot of friends, and convincing an owner you are devoted to the car's loving preservation and possess great buckets of money. Many unique body parts and trim will have to be fabricated if they need replacement; there is no old stock.

Olds' first wraparound windshield was stylish, but presents a tough replacement problem. Equipped as a virtual rolling accessory catalog, the Fiesta's various components present huge restoration challenges. Midwestern winters often did heavy damage to the car's hand-built body, so careful checks should be made for rust.

Interior fabrics and trim are best quality but very costly to redo. Many mechanical

The most common Fiesta color combination was Surf blue (back end) and Teal blue. Noel and Nile green were also offered, as were solid white and black. Interiors were finished in green, blue or black hand-buffed leather trimmed with ivory. Although some Fiestas have been found with Continental kits (exterior spare tires), experts believe they were not so produced by the factory.

parts interchange with other years and models, but this is about the only encouragement that can be offered the owner of a less-than-pristine Fiesta.

Because of a fire at the Hydra-matic plant that year, some 1953 Oldsmobiles were fitted with DynaFlow Drive. All Fiestas, however, are believed to have been equipped with Hydra-matics.

SUMMARY AND PROSPECTS

Unique, rare and open-bodied, the Fiesta has all the attributes that make collector juices flow. The few examples around cost more than $20,000, and even a basket case may run half that. On the other hand, rare cars are still being dug out of ancient barns and pried loose from the proverbial little old ladies . . . why not the odd Fiesta?

PRODUCTION

458

1953 Fiesta	
ENGINE	
Type	8-cyl 90-deg V-8, water-cooled, cast-iron block and heads
Bore x stroke	3.75x3.44 in.
Displacement	303.7 ci
Valve operation	hydraulic
Compression ratio	8.0:1
Carburetion	4-bbl downdraft
Bhp	170 gross at 3600 rpm
CHASSIS & DRIVETRAIN	
Transmission	Hydra-matic
Rear axle ratio	3.64:1
Front suspension	independent, coil springs, tube shocks
Rear suspension	live axle, coil springs, tube shocks
GENERAL	
Wheelbase	124 in.
Overall length	215 in.
Track	59 in.
Tire size	7.60x15
Weight	4,453 lb
PERFORMANCE	
Acceleration	0-60: 13 sec
Top speed	105 mph
Fuel mileage	14-18 mpg

Behind the wheel in a Fiesta, you can see the special waffle-pattern upholstery. The dash houses controls for a plethora of equipment.

And power steering and brakes, super deluxe radio, Autronic Eye (though it is not visible in this photo) and heater/defroster were standard.

Chapter 9

98 Starfire convertible

1954

HISTORY

Top of the line in the restyle year of 1954, the 98 convertible was uniformly named Starfire, after the jet fighter and, more directly, a 1953 Motorama sports special (see Chapter 30). Moving up in size, performance, glitz and luxury, Oldsmobile added two inches to the wheelbase of all models and sported Motorama-inspired styling: wraparound windshield, radical two-toning and posh interior.

To lower the cars some three inches without losing any ground clearance, the chassis-frame was completely redesigned. The Rocket engine received its first enlargement, to 324.3 ci via larger bore, giving it more gross brake horsepower.

Sales were not good in 1954, but the Starfire, which usually cost more than $3,500, still racked up a creditable number of customers. It was the first of Oldsmobile's mid-fifties land yachts.

IDENTIFICATION

"Ninety-Eight" in script above rear fender trim, "Starfire" in script above trim on front fenders.

PERFORMANCE AND UTILITY

Large, heavy, a clumsy handler but a "rocket" off the line, the Starfire is a typical mid-fifties luxury convertible with all that

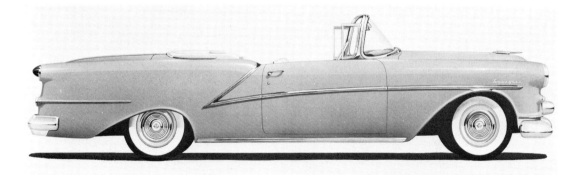

Many Fiesta styling ideas were incorporated in the 98 Starfire for 1954 which, although the most expensive Oldsmobile in the line, was priced to sell in much higher volume than the Fiesta. Production accounted for 6,800 of these classy convertibles, which was rather good going in a disappointing sales year. Hand-buffed leather interiors, a carryover from Fiesta, makes Starfires expensive to reupholster.

implies, pro and con. Ample room for six passengers in its leather-swathed interior. The cars are usually found with a raft of power options. Starfires have fairly clean styling and are solidly built.

PROBLEM AREAS

By 1954, Futuramic styling and Rocket V-8 power had evolved considerably. Larger front suspension spindles and a stronger rear axle had quelled earlier trouble spots. The 12-volt electrical system eased Rocket V-8 starting problems and helped feed the growing number of electrical accessories Olds buyers were adding to their cars.

Internal lubrication was better on the Rocket V-8, but a new inside engine problem surfaced in this era: The skirted pistons were prone to cracking. One veteran Lansing mechanic reported fishing many a detached piston skirt out of disabled Oldsmobiles' oil pans! Camshaft problems began to surface, but got worse later. Water pump failures were common in both 1954 and 1955 models.

The interiors on these convertibles are expensive to redo and there is the usual heavy competition for relatively rare external chrome goodies. The Starfire was somewhat rust-prone in its lower body area.

SUMMARY AND PROSPECTS

Not important historically, the 1954 Starfire is nevertheless a flashy, attractive, well-built car and a fine highway performer. The soft top body style guarantees it more than average appreciation in the years ahead.

PRODUCTION
6,800

1954 Starfire convertible	
ENGINE	
Type	8-cyl 90-deg V-8, water-cooled, cast-iron block and heads
Bore x stroke	3.88x3.44 in.
Displacement	324.3 ci
Valve operation	hydraulic
Compression ratio	8.25:1
Carburetion	4-bbl downdraft
Bhp	185 gross at 4000 rpm
CHASSIS & DRIVETRAIN	
Transmission	Hydra-matic
Rear axle ratio	3.42:1
Front suspension	independent, coil springs, tube shocks
Rear suspension	live axle, coil springs, tube shocks
GENERAL	
Wheelbase	126 in.
Overall length	214.3 in.
Track	59 in. front, 58 in. rear
Tire size	7.60x15
Weight	4,193 lb
PERFORMANCE	
Acceleration	0-60: 12 sec
Top speed	110 mph
Fuel mileage	12-16 mpg

The newly designed chassis-frame and heftier Rocket engine made the Starfire quicker and more solid, but the skirted pistons tended to crack, and camshaft troubles occurred too frequently to make owners happy. Lower-body rust is also a problem.

Chapter 10

98 hardtop & convertible

1955-56

★★★

HISTORY

In a stunning year for the industry, Oldsmobile surged into fourth place in both model and calendar year production behind the Big Three and Buick—a higher score than Lansing had ever enjoyed before—on the shoulders of a dramatically styled, fleet and luxurious line of 88s, Super 88s and 98s.

Though styling was only a facelift from 1954, there was a new model, one of Detroit's first four-door hardtops (a body style brought out by Cadillac the year before). Retaining its '54 dimensions, the 98 led the line, and the airy Holidays and convertibles were of course the best of the 98s. Produced in large quantities, they left the showroom for $3,000-4,500, offering comfort and luxury near the Cadillac level for about $1,000 less. In their time they were hard to resist.

GM started a major trend with the four-door hardtop, and the 98 Deluxe Holiday sedan was one of the most popular of this new body style.

Older models today tend to be loose and let in rain and dust—the immaculate low-mileage original is the one to look for, if you can find it.

IDENTIFICATION

1955: Combination bumper-grille with "floating" horizontal bar mounting "Oldsmobile" block letters in space above; parking lights mounted separately under headlamps.

1956: "Large-mouth bass" grillework combined with bumper surround. The grille bars were horizontal and split in the middle, enclosing the nameplate at right. Parking lights fared into lower bumper.

PERFORMANCE AND UTILITY

Everything from the previous chapter also applies here, only moreso. The 324 V-8 reached 202 gross bhp on the '55 98s, and 240 in 1956. Weight was pushing two tons in the latter year, with the Starfire convertible scaling 4,325 pounds at the curb. Heavy drinkers by today's standards, 98s need high-test fuel.

PROBLEM AREAS

Model-year 1956 brought the supposedly smoother Jetaway Hydra-matic transmission—at last the reliable automatic that Olds owners had been promised for years. But the Jetaway sent engineers scurrying back to their drawing boards for a quick fix. It came in subsequent years, but meanwhile a repair package was issued to dealerships.

It was not, in short, a *reliable* Hydra-matic. But it was standard equipment on 1956 98s and optional (but usually always fitted) on Super 88s. All '56s with Jetaway Hydra-matic should therefore be very carefully evalu-

The 1956 facelift was announced by a new, cleaner, combination bumper-grille. Two-toning was different along the body sides but it was still recognizably Oldsmobile. All that chrome may mean a lot of replating.

ated in this area by an expert. (See Chapter 9 for further details.)

SUMMARY AND PROSPECTS

Highly collectible today and destined to remain so. Everyone has their preference, but my choice for 1955 is the 98 four-door Holiday. I think the styling is cleaner and the two-toning less heavy. Four-door hardtops went out of favor in the seventies, but there was no denying their combination of practicality and airy sportiness. The problem was that they were looser than standard sedans.

Overall, a fine investment at today's depressed prices: $5,000 should net you a fairly decent example: $10,000 will buy you a show winner.

PRODUCTION

	1955	1956
Starfire convertible	9,149	8,581
Holiday 4-door hardtop	31,267	42,320
Holiday 2-door hardtop	38,363	19,433

1955-56 98 hardtop and convertible

ENGINE

Type	8-cyl 90-deg V-8, water-cooled, cast-iron block and heads
Bore x stroke	3.88x3.24 in.
Displacement	324.3 ci
Valve operation	hydraulic
Compression ratio	8.5:1 (1955), 9.25:1 (1956)
Carburetion	4-bbl downdraft
Bhp	202 gross at 4000 rpm (1955), 240 gross at 4400 rpm (1956)

CHASSIS & DRIVETRAIN

Transmission	Hydra-matic
Rear axle ratio	3.42:1
Front suspension	independent, coil springs, concentric tube shocks
Rear suspension	live axle, coil springs, tube shocks

GENERAL

Wheelbase	126 in.
Overall length	212.4 in.
Track	59 in. front, 58 in. rear
Tire size	7.60x15
Weight	3,924-4,167 lb

PERFORMANCE

Acceleration	0-60: 12-13 sec
Top speed	110 mph
Fuel mileage	10-15 mpg

The 324 Rocket engine belted out 240 bhp in 1956. This is a show engine with some plated parts that were not found in that condition in cars, but underhood condition is equally clean on the better Oldsmobile showcars these days.

This revised ringed-world emblem is a 1955-only piece of trim that may be difficult to find in excellent condition.

A 1955 98 Starfire convertible with optional Continental spare, owned by Don Feliciano. This and all subsequent photos of the car in this chapter are by Bud Juneau.

Headlamp treatment, which continued un-changed in 1956, was the popular Frenched approach. Those overhanging brows are rust catchers, and the backside should be checked for tinworm.

Protruding taillights mark the '55s. The smaller nacelle below is for the back-up lamps, which appear to be absent on this example.

Spinner wheel covers are not too difficult to find, but new original stock is impossible now.

The hood ornament, also unique to 1955 and accordingly scarce at swap meets.

The Continental kit extends an already over-long car but probably makes it less nose heavy. You have to admit that it makes the Starfire very dramatic. One-tone paint job, uncommon on '55s, helps clean up and set off the car's lines.

Bejeweled and dazzling, the '55 dash featured the then-popular center glovebox, but retained old-time symmetry in placement of instruments and clock.

Close-up of the Continental kit, the spare resting on a huge hunk of sheet metal and the bumper held an extra foot away from its normal position. A big chunk of iron.

Two more bits of minor trim from the front fender that will give collectors headaches finding. Pot metal pits and is hard to replate permanently once the pitting has begun.

Chapter 11

Super 88 hardtop & convertible

★★★

1955-56

HISTORY

Compared to the big 98, the Super 88 rode a four-inch-shorter wheelbase and weighed about 150-200 pounds less. Since it packed the same engine, with 17 bhp more than the baseline 88, it was the quickest and nimblest Oldsmobile model at that time. It was also the most popular, available

The shorter wheelbase isn't much apparent in the convertible model, which looks good in one tone (which was far more common on convertibles than other models).

in five different models, and accounting for well over 200,000 units in the '55 model-year and over 150,000 in '56.

Prices for the posh and comprehensively equipped convertibles and Holidays started at $2,714, but few left the showroom for under $3,500.

The four-door hardtop really came of age in 1956, when Olds sold six of them to every four two-door hardtops. In 1955 the ratio had been just about the reverse.

IDENTIFICATION

1955: Supers can be distinguished from base 88s by their rocker panel bright molding; convertible 88s came only as Supers.

1956: Super 88s had a bright molding below the side windows along the beltline, whereas standard 88s did not. Again, the convertibles were all Supers.

PERFORMANCE AND UTILITY

More fun to drive than the 98, though only marginally quicker, the Super 88 was a very typical American car then: fast off the line, thirsty except at 50 mph cruising speeds, and none too graceful on twisting roads. Plenty of room for six passengers and their luggage, and remarkably good visibility thanks to the pillarless construction of the Holiday models, and Olds' widely wrapped windshield. Hydra-matic was standard, power steering and brakes common.

PROBLEM AREAS

A GM air-conditioning system could be ordered on either the 1955 or 1956 Super 88 hardtop. Although rare and desirable, it can provide restoration problems. Interior plastic parts are impossible to find, as are some exotic interior fabrics. The padded dash was an option, but very vulnerable to sun damage. (See also Chapter 10.)

SUMMARY AND PROSPECTS

Same as 1955-56 98s (see Chapter 10). Being more common, the Super 88s are in fairly good supply compared to the 98s, but prices seem little different between the two models, and value is really determined by condition. A pillared four-door sedan and a two-door sedan were offered, but are not recommended as collectible.

Pleated, two-toned leather interior typified the open Oldsmobiles of this era. A lot of small brightmetal trim pieces abound, making restorations more complicated than on the '54 models. Virtually all Olds were now bought with whitewalls, and look naked without them.

1955-56 Super 88 hardtop and convertible
ENGINE
As per 1955-56 98
CHASSIS & DRIVETRAIN
As per 1955-56 98
GENERAL
Wheelbase .... 122 in.
Overall length .... 203.4 in.
Track .... 59 in. front, 58 in. rear
Tire size 7.60x15
Weight .... 3,765-4,083 lb
PERFORMANCE
Acceleration .... 0-60: 11-12 sec
Top speed .... 110 mph
Fuel mileage .... 12-16 mpg

PRODUCTION	*1955*	*1956*
convertible	9,007	9,561
Holiday 4-door hardtop	47,385	61,192
Holiday 2-door hardtop	62,534	43,054

Revised two-toning and scoop grille marked the 1956 models. The standard wheel cover was spinnerless, but the popular X-2 deluxe spinners cost only $38.95 per set.

The Super 88 Holiday hardtop, a lower-priced alternative to the more expensive convertible, was usually found two-toned. Big square trunk was an Oldsmobile selling point, and still comes in handy.

The Holiday version outsold the convertible by nearly four to one. It is easier to own and restore today. Air conditioning was available, though not often seen. Replacement of the clear plastic interior tubes is difficult. Colorful vinyl and fabric interiors are also difficult to replicate exactly.

Chapter 12

Golden Rocket 88/ Super 88 hardtop, convertible & Fiesta

★★★★

1957

HISTORY

The streamlined and flashy '57 GM re-style was particularly effective at Oldsmobile, which emerged clean and fresh looking. There was a new, larger engine; a perimeter frame; a new, wider-track chassis with fourteen- instead of fifteen-inch wheels; and ball-joint front suspension instead of king pins.

The Super 88 was again distinct from the 88 while sharing the same wheelbase, but both were called Golden Rocket, after a contemporary Motorama show car. There was less difference between them then, since each used the 277 hp 371 engine and each offered a convertible. For these rea-

Stylists tried to maintain a design relationship with earlier models in 1957, though all '57s were called Golden Rockets. The scoop grille and ringed-world emblem were retained, as were spinner-type wheel covers. The 88s were a physically smaller car and were more fun to drive. As usual, the top investment is the convertible model.

sons, the 1957 88 is probably more collectible than the clumsier and bulkier 98.

Incidentally, though GM was officially out of racing, a young NASCAR driver ran a Golden Rocket 88 on the oval circuits that year: His name was Richard Petty.

IDENTIFICATION

Scoop-type bumper-grille carried the Oldsmobile name in individual letters; round parking lights at extreme grille edges. Frenched headlamps were surmounted with small rocket-type mascots. On 88s, the curved body molding started at the center post; on Super 88s, it swept backward from a point farther forward. Neither model used a bright molding on the rocker panel.

PERFORMANCE AND UTILITY

Although it offered tremendous straight-line performance, the 1957 Oldsmobile was, as Jan Norbye (in his *Oldsmobile: The Postwar Years*) put it, "a soft car to drive, with sloppy springs and body motions that caused seasickness in many passengers." Its weaknesses included slow and imprecise steering, excessive suspension bounce and extreme body roll. Quality had also begun to deteriorate in 1957, though not as markedly at GM as at Ford or Chrysler.

PROBLEM AREAS

This car's engine was probably the most problem-beset of the first generation of this normally reliable powerplant. Camshafts regularly failed, lifters were often noisy. Frequent oil changes are a must on '57s; since not all their owners realized that, it is rare to find one that has not had top-end engine work.

A Super 88 Holiday owned by Michael Cromer typifies this big, handsome series for 1957. This and the subsequent photos in this chapter are by Bud Juneau.

This model-year brought the split drive shaft, which was prone to vibration and early failure of the center bearing.

Chrome trim, emblems and interior fabric and trim are very hard to come by. Bumpers were rust catchers, and replacements (even in replatable condition) are scarce. Through-the-bumper exhaust tips were stylish, but are troublesome to restore to like-new condition.

The increasing amount of chrome trim and emblems are a restoration problem on '57s because they are extremely scarce. Often very large components, such as bumpers, have to be replaced because of rust.

Trademark rockets, so long on the hood, now were moved to the fender tops; spares are difficult to find in decent condition, since they were only around for a year. And you'll need two of them. . . .

SUMMARY AND PROSPECTS

At the time, Olds Division didn't consider this car a hit: Production for '57 dropped behind the '56 pace. And while Olds retained fifth place in sales, its share of the market

A popular fad of the era was exhaust outlets in the bumpers. Cromer's car is spotless in this respect, but the outlets require constant attention and the area around them needs to be cleaned frequently.

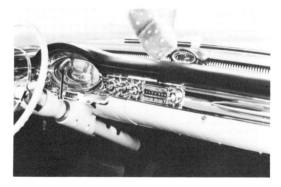

Fuzzy dice are a cute touch of contemporary nostalgia. Garish dashboard is no fun in convertibles.

was down by over one percent. But latter-day collectors have given the Golden Rockets a lot of popularity. They certainly had more luxury and gadgets than any of their predecessors.

The reborn Olds wagon, the Fiesta, is historically important, and its hardtop version interesting. Shoppers should take care to avoid the more common body styles: The ones listed here will, I think, remain sound values with decent appreciation—especially if they have the J-2 engine, which I'll discuss in Chapter 13.

PRODUCTION	88	Super 88
Holiday 2-door hardtop	49,187	31,155
Holiday 4-door hardtop	33,830	39,162
convertible	6,423	7,128
Fiesta wagon	5,052	—
Fiesta hardtop wagon	5,767	8,981

(2-door and 4-door sedans not recommended)

1957 Golden Rocket

ENGINE
Type ..... 8-cyl 90-deg V-8, water-cooled, cast-iron block and heads
Bore x stroke .... 4.00x3.69 in.
Displacement .... 371.1 ci
Valve operation .... hydraulic
Compression ratio 3.64:1
Carburetion .... Quadrajet 4-bbl downdraft
Bhp .... 277 gross at 4400 rpm
CHASSIS & DRIVETRAIN
Transmission .... Hydra-matic
Rear axle ratio 3.64:1
Front suspension ... independent, coil springs, concentric tube shocks
Rear suspension .... live axle, coil springs, tube shocks
GENERAL
Wheelbase .... 122 in.
Overall length .... 208.2 in.
Track .... 59 in. front, 58 in. rear
Tire size 8.50x14
Weight .... 3,942-4,364 lb
PERFORMANCE
Acceleration .... 0-60: 10-12 sec
Top speed .... 110-115 mph
Fuel mileage .... 11-15 mpg

Hood ornaments were almost passe by now, and Oldsmobile's had become highly stylized—another scarce trim item, this, as is the emblem below it.

Things would be easier if the cars wore the same badge fore and aft, but the deck version carries a keyhole and is contoured differently.

Trisected backlight was an interesting styling feature, though the unnecessary extra pillars present a small visibility handicap.

The '57 was a glamorous-looking car but beset with some serious mechanical problems. Single-tone paint jobs were regaining popularity and, I think improve the look of the car compared to two-tones.

Chapter 13

Golden Rocket/ Starfire J-2

1957

HISTORY

If the new 371 V-8 for 1957 still wasn't enough, Oldsmobile had your answer in January of that year: The even more potent J-2 engine, with a special manifold mounting triple two-barrel carburetors, and a cylinder head-gasket kit which brought compression ratio from 9.5:1 to 10:1. Remarkably, the J-2

Salient features of the J-2 were the special manifold, triple two-barrel carburetors and higher compression through a cylinder head gasket kit. This option costs only $83 extra. J-2 Golden Rockets of all body styles are hot items among today's collectors, but they're not commonplace.

option cost only $83.

Yet more esoteric was the competition J-2, which added a high-lift cam, racing pistons and other beefed-up internal parts at a modest $385. This engine was almost unknown in street machines, however.

IDENTIFICATION

88s and Super 88s as per Chapter 12. 98s had a brightmetal applique over rocker panels. The J-2 engine may easily be identified by popping the hood: Look for multiple carburetion.

PERFORMANCE AND UTILITY

Motor Trend tested a J-2 98 and did 0-60 in 9.4 seconds; well-broken-in 98s could cut half a second off that, and 88s were capable of the spring in under eight seconds. Oldsmobile claimed that the J-2 was perfectly economical when you kept your foot off it, since it then ran on only one carburetor, and of course all J-2 drivers carefully kept their feet off. (And if you will believe *that*, you will believe *anything*.)

PROBLEM AREAS

The J-2 package did not present any additional problems, but hard driving *did* compound the normal '57 cam and lifter troubles. J-2 restorers can find used carburetors and intake manifolds, but may be stumped by carb linkage, air cleaners and paper elements for the same. (See also Chapter 12.)

SUMMARY AND PROSPECTS

J-2 '57s are some of the hottest Oldsmobiles among collectors today. And as long as they can run without trouble, they will probably remain so. (Despite the ruckus collectors raised when the lead went out, it seems to cause no damage.) The option was available across the board, so it may be found on 98s as well. The ideal combination would be the J-2 engine in a low-mileage original-condition Super 88 convertible. Such a formula will spin a $30,000 price tag in a few years.

PRODUCTION
Unknown

1957 J-2

ENGINE

Type . . . . . 8-cyl 90-deg V-8, water-cooled, cast-iron block and heads
Bore x stroke . . . . 4.00x3.69 in.
Displacement . . . . 371.1 ci
Valve operation . . . . hydraulic
Compression ratio 10.0:1
Carburetion . . . . triple 2-bbl downdraft
Bhp . . . . 312 gross at 4600 rpm

CHASSIS & DRIVETRAIN

As per standard 1957 models (see Chapters 11 & 12)

GENERAL

As per standard 1957 models (see Chapters 11 & 12)

PERFORMANCE

Acceleration . . . . 0-60: 8-9 sec
Top speed . . . . 120 mph
Fuel mileage . . . . 7-12 mpg

COMPETITION VERSION

Not offered to the public, this competition J-2 offered full-race camshaft, heavy-duty pistons and beefed internals for $385

Chapter 14

98 hardtop & convertible
1958

★

HISTORY

Why not be perverse here, and select the biggest and clumsiest of the clumsy batch of cars as the outstanding contender in the Ugly Olds contest. But of course, it's easy to be wise in hindsight. In 1958, chrome sold cars,

There is no middle ground on the '58s. If you're going to own one, I recommend the flashiest 98s, such as this Holiday hardtop, with even more chrome and brushed stainless steel than the 88s had. Note the wheel covers, which are color-keyed to the top color.

or so it was thought when the '58s were designed in 1955-56. Oldsmobile, facing a revived Dodge and tough Pontiac/Mercury competition at the bottom end of its market, was looking to move upward into that same elusive territory also beckoning such makes as Edsel and DeSoto. And we all know what happened to them.

Wandering around Lansing, asking who designed the 1958 Oldsmobile is like old Diogenes with his lantern, searching for an honest man. Art Ross has been known to acknowledge some furtive responsibility. Bill Mitchell denies he ever set foot in the Olds studio. Alex Tremulis, who worked for Ford, drew a '58 with a cleft sign and little musical notes pasted to its rear fender speed lines. Such a thing should have been an option for Liberace!

Engineeringwise, New-Matic air-sprung suspension ought to be mentioned: It will not be found on many '58s because it was quite unpopular in its day. Many cars that started with it have since been converted to conventional springs, owing to its unreliable air chambers and difficult-to-find parts. The 98 is also recommended in the overkill category because it had a newer and larger V-8, 394 ci, the biggest yet, with 315 bhp. (The powerplant was also an option in the Super 88.)

IDENTIFICATION
Unmistakable. Lollipop taillights, a triple band of speed lines over a rocketlike bulge on the rear fender, more speed lines and much chrome along the front fender and door. "Ninety Eight" script on front fender.

PERFORMANCE AND UTILITY
Performance on par with previous year's model: 0-60 in about eleven to twelve seconds, a top speed far too high for its brakes and suspension. Most examples laden with power accessories, as they ought to be.

PROBLEM AREAS
Known as the Chrome King, the top-of-the-line '58 will give a restorer fits finding replacement brightwork, just because of the shear volume required. Rather exotic interior fabrics can add heavily to the restoration bill.

The air suspension (New-Matic Ride) caused major woes; a dealer kit eliminated it from most cars so equipped. If your car has it, check it carefully for leaks.

The convertible version weighed two tons and the typical model sold for close to $5,000, big money in those days. Only 5,605 were produced.

Color-coordinated wheel covers were offered in five different colors to match or (as in this case) contrast the body colors.

SUMMARY AND PROSPECTS

Not moving fast in popularity or value, the '58 is really an instrument of inverse snob appeal. (A stylist whom I know drives the counterpart Buick Limited, charcoal and pink, to his Detroit office every day for the fun of it. He is really much better than that, too.) An interesting artifact of a period in history. You might find the most amazing example for little more than its cost when new.

PRODUCTION

Holiday 2-door hardtop	11,012
Holiday 4-door hardtop	27,603
convertible	5,605
(sedan not recommended)	

Another popular fifties theme was the confusion-drill hidden gas filler. The average '58 took on a lot of gas over its lifetime, and surrounding chrome parts are often well scratched or dinged.

Plenty of stainless steel was used, which tends not to trouble collectors, but there was still enough chrome to cover a dozen lesser cars, and the large fender caps were pure pot metal.

1958 98

ENGINE
Type	8-cyl 90-deg V-8, water-cooled, cast-iron block and heads
Bore x stroke	4.00x3.69 in.
Displacement	371.1 ci
Valve operation	hydraulic
Compression ratio	10.0:1
Carburetion	Quadrajet downdraft
Bhp	305 gross at 4600 rpm

CHASSIS & DRIVETRAIN
Transmission	Hydra-matic
Rear axle ratio	3.42:1
Front suspension	independent, coil springs, concentric tube shocks
Rear suspension	live axle, 4-link, coil springs, tube shocks

GENERAL
Wheelbase	126.5 in.
Overall length	216.7 in.
Track	59 in. front, 58 in. rear
Tire size	8.50x14
Weight	4,316-4,391 lb

PERFORMANCE
Acceleration	0-60: 12-13 sec
Top speed	110 mph
Fuel mileage	12-14 mpg

You'll not be able to raise that massive hood from this position. Huge amounts of chrome make a '58 a formidable restoration, and it will probably cost more than the car will ever be worth. Clean originals are the answer here.

Chapter 15

Starfire
1961-66

★ ★ ★ ★	convertible
★ ★ ★	hardtop

HISTORY

Under Bill Mitchell, who took over GM Styling in 1958, the cars quickly abandoned the age of jukebox design for a clean, extruded look, though Mitchell took care—which today's GM does not—to keep divisional design separate and, to some extent, competitive. Oldsmobile developed its own look, and with that, a limited edition, taking the Starfire name again.

First it was a convertible only, with a special engine, deluxe interior and a host of standard luxuries, identified by its broad band of bodyside stainless steel. A hardtop was added in 1962, and became the only body style in 1966, after which it disappeared—displaced by the Toronado as the "personal luxury" Oldsmobile.

The first Starfire, 1961, showed a trace of Harley Earl's influence in its distinctive brushed-aluminum side panel, though Mitchell liked these too.

Issued only as a convertible this year, it saw 7,800 copies, which was a lot compared to the volume in subsequent years.

IDENTIFICATION

Broad stainless steel body paneling marks the 1961-62 model. It became narrower in 1963 and was dropped in 1964, when Starfires were marked by a "trident" in chrome just behind the front wheel arches. The 1965 model was almost indistinguishable from any other senior Olds (but carried "Starfire" lettering on the front fenders), while the single coupe model in 1966 got a bit of stainless back—in a panel running low on the body sides, carrying dummy scoops on the front fenders.

PERFORMANCE AND UTILITY

Exceptional in 1961 with the 325 hp engine in a Dynamic 88 shell, it gradually became quite ordinary as the years passed and the full-size Oldsmobile became heavier —but it never lost the 123 inch wheelbase. Another jumbo land cruiser, with bucket seats and console after '61, most of them were fitted with all the power options and, of course, Hydra-matic. A comfortable, easy-to-drive but thirsty and fairly clumsy handling model.

PROBLEM AREAS

Lack of leaded fuel could impact this model. Water pump failure was prevalent. New 1964 Slim-Jim transmissions were not reliable. Stainless side trim is very vulnerable and nearly impossible to find. Premium interiors are expensive to fix.

SUMMARY AND PROSPECTS

Similar in concept to the early Buick Rivieras, but not nearly as exclusive, the Starfire tends to appeal to dyed-in-the-wool Oldsmobile types who know enough to be discerning. It will never possess the prestige and desirability of a Riviera, but it remains one of the most coveted big Oldsmobiles— especially the scarce convertible models.

Prices are relatively reasonable (much lower than Rivieras). A slow increase in value can be expected for hardtops; the rare convertibles are already moving rapidly. Though more numerous, the 1961-62 convertibles are at least as desirable as the later models, owing to their many special features.

The Hardtop arrived in 1962, along with detail styling changes. Easy identification is by the side panel louvers, which moved back to the door this year.

PRODUCTION	1961	1962	1963	1964	1965	1966
convertible	7,800	7,149	4,401	2,410	2,236	—
hardtop	—	34,839	21,148	13,753	13,024	13,019

Only 4,401 1963 Starfire convertibles were built, though hardtop production was high. Bucket seats, console, automatic transmission, along with power brakes, windows and seats were standard.

Brushed-aluminum band was much thinner on 1963 Starfire. Extruded, creased styling was a hallmark of the Mitchell era.

1961-66 Starfire

ENGINE

Type . . . . . 8-cyl 90-deg V-8, water-cooled, cast-iron block and heads
Bore x stroke . . . 4.13x3.69 in. (1961-64), 4.13x3.98 in. (1965-66)
Displacement . . . . 394 ci (1961-64), 425 ci (1965-66)
Valve operation . . . . hydraulic
Compression ratio 10:1 (1961-62), 10.5:1 (1963-66)
Carburetion . . . . Quadrajet downdraft
Bhp . . . . 325 (1961-62), 345 (1963-64) gross at 3600 rpm; 370 (1965), 375 (1966) gross at 4800 rpm

CHASSIS & DRIVETRAIN

Transmission . . . . Hydra-matic
Rear axle ratio 3.42:1 (1961-64), 3.23:1 (1965-66)

Front suspension . . . independent, coil springs, concentric tube shocks
Rear suspension . . . . live axle, 4-link, coil springs, tube shocks

GENERAL

Wheelbase . . . . 123 in.
Overall length . . . . 179.3-179.6 in.
Track . . . . 61/61 in. (1961-62), 62.2/61 in. (1963-64), 62/64 in. (1965-66)
Tire size 8.00x14 (1961-64), 8.25x14 (1965-66)
Weight . . . . 2,736-2,983 lb

PERFORMANCE

Acceleration . . . . 0-60 (ave): 9-11 sec
Top speed . . . . 115-120 mph (ave)
Fuel mileage . . . . 12-15 mpg (ave)

Aluminum side panel was finally dropped on the '64s, but a chrome trident decoration gave quick identification. From this point on, collectibility diminishes.

Aside from lettering on fenders, it was hard to
tell the '65 Starfire from a standard Olds, though
interior remained sumptuous.

Aluminum trim came back in 1966, the last year,
but the convertible was dropped and hardtop
production was at its lowest, just over 13,000.

Chapter 16

F-85 Cutlass
1961-63

★★	convertible
★	coupe

HISTORY

Oldsmobile's compact was based on a shared bodyshell with the Buick Special and Pontiac Tempest but—and again in contrast to GM today—each car had its distinct differences and personality. Olds' F-85 came only with a V-8, the aluminum 215 built by Buick. Its styling was cleaner and less busy than Buick's, and its prices a shade lower.

Following the unexpected success of the Corvair Monza, all GM compacts quickly added "sports" models with bucket seats and luxury interiors. Oldsmobile's Cutlass was an upgrade of the basic F-85 coupe, which itself wasn't offered until mid model year.

There was no doubt that the formula worked: The Cutlass outsold the plain coupe five cars to one. A convertible model

Most desirable '61 Cutlass is the bucket-seated sports coupe. First-year status gives the '61 sports coupe an edge, but the economy coupe model is far less collectible.

was added in 1962, by which time Cutlasses owned the lion's share of F-85 sales. The neat little F-85 was drastically changed in 1964, however. Its replacement was not quite as singular looking, although quicker.

Naming the Olds compact was a process fraught with controversy. "Starfire" was suggested, then dropped because of its big-car connotations. "Rockette" failed because it suggested Radio City dancers. "F-85" stemmed from a show car called F-88, minus three digits to avoid confusion with the 88 line. Namewise, it was like the camel—a horse designed by a committee.

IDENTIFICATION

1961: Vertical-blade grille surmounting "Oldsmobile" letters. Cutlass had chrome trim around side windows and chrome spear along bodysides.

1962: Name moved to hood, bright horizontal bar inset on grille. Cutlass had chrome rocker molding.

1963: More massive front bumper encompassing parking lights. Mesh grille carried Oldsmobile name in meshless horizontal center section. "Cutlass" script on all.

PERFORMANCE AND UTILITY

Sprightly performance and good economy were F-85 features. Power was up in 1962, when 185 bhp power-pack version of the Buick 215 was standard on Cutlass. This was raised to 195 bhp on the 1963 model. Strictly a four-passenger car, and not much room in the back. Fun to drive with stick transmission. Contemporary packaging for a rear-drive car. An improved dash made the '63 model nicer yet.

PROBLEM AREAS

This was the smallest car built on an Oldsmobile assembly line in many years, and early models had the usual start-up bugs. The biggest problems came under the hood, however: The aluminum small-block was a good design and an easy unit to work on, but there were metallurgic difficulties. Chemical reactions between engine metals and the heater-core elements caused problems even while the cars were under new-car warranty. Leakage and corrosion were also common on the engine, and some had a tendency toward rough running.

The survival rate of the early Cutlasses

This and subsequent photos are of the 1962 F-85 Cutlass convertible owned by Bill and Marge Bush. Photography by Bud Juneau.

Vertical bar grilles decorated early F-85s; this one has minor dings, but new-old-stock replacements are very scarce.

seems very low. There were general body rust problems, so a careful check by the prospective buyer is recommended.

SUMMARY AND PROSPECTS

Not nearly as hot a collectible as the Jetfire variation (see Chapter 17), but perhaps ideal as a combination hobby car and occasional family transporter. The Cutlass is very affordable, and clean originals should not cost more than the down payment on a new model. No great prospects for fast value appreciation, these cars are for having fun without spending a fortune. The convertible is, of course, much more desirable than the coupe.

PRODUCTION	1961	1962	1963
sport coupe	9,935	32,461	41,343
convertible	—	9,893	12,149

1961-63 F-85 Cutlass

ENGINE
Type .... 90-deg V-8, water-cooled, cast-iron block and heads
Bore x stroke .... 3.50x2.80 in.
Displacement .... 215 ci
Valve operation .... hydraulic
Compression ratio 8.5:1 (1961), 10.25:1 (1962-63)
Carburetion .... downdraft; 2-bbl (1961), 4-bbl (1962-63)
Bhp .... 155 gross (1961), 185 gross (1962-63) at 4800 rpm
CHASSIS & DRIVETRAIN
Transmission .... 3-spd, Hydra-matic opt
Rear axle ratio .... 3.08:1, 3.23:1 (automatic)
Front suspension ...... independent, coil springs, tube shocks
Rear suspension .. link-type, live axle, coil springs, tube shocks
GENERAL
Wheelbase .... 112 in.
Overall length .... 188 in. (1962), 192 in. (1963)
Track .... 56 in.
Tire size 6.50x13
Weight .... 2,650 lb, 2,850 lb (convertible)
PERFORMANCE
Acceleration .... 13 sec
Top speed .... 95 mph
Fuel mileage .... 16-19 mpg

Cutlass dash was fairly Spartan; clock would go in square space to right of speedo; warning lights governed ampere and oil pressure messages.

Console with gear selecter stalk (for Hydramatic in this car) and bucket seats were a mark of upscale Cutlass models. Vinyl dashboard trim cracks and is difficult to repair.

The 185 bhp V-8 is a fairly tight squeeze, gave good performance but occasional service problems through metallurgic difficulties.

F-85 received longer, wider body in 1963, and some Olds collectors say this cost it individuality. Package looks very up to date, though, nearly a quarter-century later.

Cutlass convertible was a clean design that still looks modern; soft top model is worth at least 75 percent more than a coupe in comparable condition.

F-85 Jetfire
1961-63

 ★★★★

HISTORY

On paper, it looked good. Conventional power modifications to the aluminum 215 V-8 were difficult—compression couldn't be raised, more carbs and a hotter camshaft would disrupt smoothness and the good low-end torque. One of the big Olds engines would be too heavy. Gilbert Burrell, who had come up with the original Rocket V-8, opted for a turbocharger, collaborating with Olds engineers Ed Rosetti, Ted Louckes, Gibson Butler and Frank Ball.

The conventional centrifugal blower was built for Olds by AiResearch. To get the engine to tolerate it, and the 10.25:1 compression ratio it entailed, the designers added an injection system for Turbo Rocket Fluid (half distilled water, half methyl alcohol) stored

Supercharger was conventional Roots type, but injection system used a distilled water and methyl alcohol combination, which was unorthodox. This is a polished show engine.

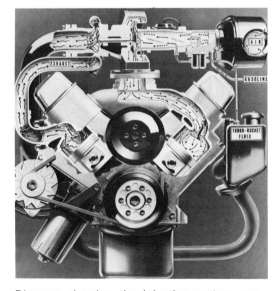

Diagram showing the injection system combination of incoming air and Turbo-Rocket Fluid led to supercharger for combustion and exhaust.

Studio shot of the Jetfire with see-through hood
showing blown engine. Note brushed-aluminum
side trim, exclusive to this model.

in a pressure reservoir and injected commensurate with turbo boost starting at 1 psi. This fluid-injection not only prevented ping, but also added somewhat to power output, thanks to the methyl alcohol.

It was an interesting though complex solution to the need for increased performance, and it certainly produced jolting acceleration. But the system wasn't reliable, and was abandoned after the 1963 model year.

IDENTIFICATION

Brushed aluminum side trim was a Jetfire exclusive, as were Jetfire badges on the fenders. Year-to-year identification was the same as for the 1962-63 Cutlass.

PERFORMANCE AND UTILITY

A superb performer, the Jetfire typically scores 0-60 in about 8.5 seconds, with a top speed of about 110 mph; yet it will deliver reasonable fuel economy if you can manage to stay off the turbo boost. Bucket seats and console restrict passenger capacity to four; rear seating is cramped.

PROBLEM AREAS

The water-injection turbocharger system was subject to faults even when under warranty, and it is not any more reliable now. Carbon buildup was a problem with Jetfire engines.

Many of the turbocharging and fluid-injection systems were removed entirely or partially disconnected. If buying a Jetfire, the prospective owner should make sure everything is there, and that it works. As with any turbocharged engine, the miles take their toll.

Brushed stainless side trim is just as much a problem here as on the contemporary Starliner. (See also Chapter 16.)

SUMMARY AND PROSPECTS

A unique, low-volume car with singular performance, the F-85 Jetfire remains one of the most desirable Oldsmobiles, regardless of its reliability problems. Jetfires are worth about triple the value of standard Cutlasses in similar condition, and will continue to appreciate strongly.

Jetfire production was much higher in 1963, but at the overall low level it did not pay to keep on building them; the trend to bigger compact car engines also contributed to the Jetfire's demise.

PRODUCTION	*1962*	*1963*
sport coupe	3,765	5,842

1962-63 Jetfire

ENGINE
Type .... 90-deg V-8, water-cooled, cast-iron block and heads
Bore x stroke .... 3.50x2.80 in.
Displacement .... 215 ci
Valve operation .... hydraulic
Compression ratio 10.0:1
Carburetion .... 4-bbl downdraft
Bhp .... 215 gross at 4600 rpm

CHASSIS & DRIVETRAIN
Transmission .... 3-spd, Hydra-matic opt
Rear axle ratio .... 3.08:1, 3.23:1 with automatic
Front suspension ...... independent, coil springs, tube shocks
Rear suspension .. link-type, live axle, coil springs, tube shocks

GENERAL
Wheelbase .... 112 in.
Overall length .... 118 in. (1962), 192 in. (1963)
Track .... 56 in.
Tire size 6.50x13
Weight .... 2,739-2,774 lb

PERFORMANCE
Acceleration .... 0-60: 8.5 sec
Top speed .... 110 mph
Fuel mileage .... 14-18 mpg

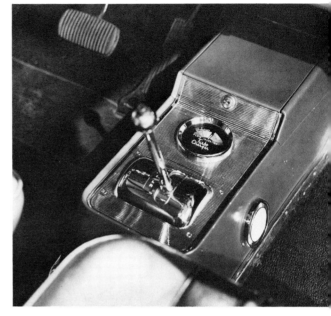

Console-housed gauge kept the driver informed of boost level, and included a green economy zone.

Vista Cruiser
1964-67

HISTORY

High style isn't common on station wagons, but some have it, witness the 1955-57 Chevy Nomad. Olds' neatest wagon of the sixties was the Vista Cruiser, with its raised, tinted-glass roof panels, possibly inspired by the aluminum Vista-Dome streamlined rail passenger cars. Lansing built Vista Cruisers from 1964 well into the 1970s, but the nicest

are the early ones, built before emission controls began to affect performance, and styling entered a clumsy stage.

All too typically, what is collectible today was unpopular when new. People tended to look upon wagons as utilitarian vehicles, and like those early Nomads the Vista Cruisers didn't sell. Styling was clean and neat, and performance was excellent, but the average

Unlikely collectible, the Vista Cruiser was the most imaginative station wagon since Chevy's Nomad. This 1964 model holds an entire first-string Little League team.

Vista Cruiser cost $200 or $300 more than a conventional wagon, and few people could see its value.

Perhaps inevitably, sales began to increase as the car's size got larger in the late sixties. (Many people don't realize the Vista Cruiser is physically larger than the F-85 wagon.) Yet the line remained a cross between intermediate and full-size Oldsmobile, on its own wheelbase.

IDENTIFICATION

1964: Horizontal bar grille, name on hood.

1965: Similar grille but name then incorporated on main grille bar.

1966: Heavier body styling, massive single-bar grille with rocket emblem centered.

1967: Parking lights moved from bumper to fit between quad headlights, creating narrower grille bar.

PERFORMANCE AND UTILITY

Performance adequate with the V-8, which was always standard on Vista Cruiser wagons. Excellent space utilization and plenty of cargo space. Unlike the standard F-85s, Vista Cruisers were mounted on a longer, 120 inch wheelbase (F-85s, 115 inches), which made them almost standard-size cars. This approximate wheelbase was retained through 1974, after which the Vista Cruiser became a body style within the shorter Cutlass series.

Styling was changed in detail on the 1965 model. The distinctive tinted sky-view panels on rear roof are thought to have been inspired by Vista-Dome railroad cars.

PROBLEM AREAS

Fairly bulletproof mechanically, this is an easy car to restore and maintain. There was some tendency toward rust, even around the rooftop Vista section, and brakes weren't great—the wagon's added weight compounded the problem here.

A restorer may find exclusive-to-Vista-Cruiser parts and trim hard to find. Many led workhorse lives, and interiors in particular didn't hold up well in hard use.

SUMMARY AND PROSPECTS

Frankly, I had no idea how rare these cars were until I looked up the production figures—which, among the standard models, are lower than the Nomad's. This is not to say they will ever become as desirable as the latter, which are far more unique and came in a vintage three years for Chevrolet. But it *does* suggest that the early Vista Cruisers are definite sleepers, with some potential for appreciation. Try to find the cleanest original you can—restoration expense is just not warranted by the end value, at least for now.

1964-67 F-85 Vista Cruiser

ENGINE

Type	90-deg V-8, water-cooled, cast-iron block and heads
Bore x stroke	3.94x3.38 in.
Displacement	330 ci
Valve operation	hydraulic
Compression ratio	9.0:1, 10.25:1 opt
Carburetion	downdraft; 2-bbl, 4-bbl opt
Bhp	230 gross at 4400 rpm (1964), 250 gross at 4800 rpm (1965-67), 320 gross at 5200 rpm (opt 1966-67)

CHASSIS & DRIVETRAIN

Transmission	3-spd, Hydra-matic opt
Rear axle ratio	3.08:1, 3.23:1 (automatic)
Front suspension	independent, coil springs, tube shocks
Rear suspension	link-type, live axle, coil springs, tube shocks

GENERAL

Wheelbase	120 in.
Overall length	208 in.
Track	58 in. (1964-65); 58 in. front, 59 in. rear (1966-67)
Tire size	7.50x14 (1964), 7.75x14 (1965), 8.25x14 (1966-67)
Weight	3,652-3,907 lb

PERFORMANCE

Acceleration	0-60: 12-15 sec
Top speed	90-95 mph
Fuel mileage	13-17 mpg

PRODUCTION	1964	1965	1966	1967
Standard 6-passenger	1,305	2,110	1,660	—
Standard 8-passenger	2,089	3,335	1,869	2,748
Custom 6-passenger	—	—	8,910	9,513
Custom 8-passenger	—	—	14,164	15,293

By far the most common Vista Cruiser is the 1966 Custom eight-passenger model. Standard models (less brightwork, more plebian interiors) are extremely rare but not in demand.

Production was highest in Vista Cruiser's last year of 1967. This is a six-passenger version of the Custom, of which 9,513 were built. Much rarer pre-1965 models are more collectible.

Chapter 19

F-85 Cutlass 4-4-2
1964-65

★★★★★ ★★★★	convertible coupe

HISTORY

Planned by Chief Engineer Harold Metzel, who later succeeded Jack Wolfram as Division general manager, the 4-4-2 was Oldsmobile's response to the popular Pontiac GTO. Early 4-4-2s were an option package, not a separate model; much of the initial B-9 4-4-2 package came right from the F-85 "police" package.

The name stood for four speeds, four-

The 4-4-2 was an option package in its first year, shown here on the Cutlass coupe for 1964. Badge is on lower front fender. Red-stripe tires, pseudo wire wheels, rarely found, are hotly desired today.

barrel carburetor and dual exhausts. The original '64 came with a hot 330 ci V-8, heavy-duty suspension and a four-speed manual gearbox as standard. In 1965 it was hotter still with the 400 V-8, an underbored version of the 425 used in large Oldsmobiles.

The 4-4-2 option package inclusive of four-speed cost only about $250 over the base Cutlass Deluxe in 1965, which was quite a bargain. It included heavy-duty wheels, shocks, springs, rear axle, drive shaft, engine mounts, steering and frame, stabilizer bars front and rear, fat tires, special exterior and interior trim, eleven-inch clutch, and a 70-amp/hr battery. Performance was sizzling, proving, as *Motor Trend* recorded, that "Detroit can build cars that perform, handle and stop, without sacrificing road comfort."

IDENTIFICATION

1964: Horizontal bar grille, name on hood, 4-4-2 badges. Some cars equipped with wire wheel covers and dummy knock-off hubs, which are very desirable today.

1965: Name incorporated in main grille bar. Model is easily identified by a C-shaped speed molding just ahead of the rear wheel arches, containing the 4-4-2 badge.

PERFORMANCE AND UTILITY

A very serious performer: In 1964, 0-60 took 7.5 seconds, less in 1965. The standing quarter mile was done in no more than seventeen seconds at no less than 85 mph, and the top speed was about 125 mph. Fuel mileage was everything this kind of power suggested, and nobody minded much. It may be more of a problem today, when octanes are more limited. Excellent handlers on all types of roads, but they have a pretty stiff ride, despite what *Motor Trend* said.

PROBLEM AREAS

A strong car but, like other hot Oldsmobiles, 4-4-2s saw extremely hard use,

Detail styling revisions followed on the 1965 model; 4-4-2 badge moved to rear fender inside scoop. This was a hotter car, with the new 400 ci V-8.

especially in Stoplight Grand Prix. Brakes were the weakest part of the package. Underhood, the '64 was the only 4-4-2 to use the 330 ci engine. Water pumps were subject to early failure.

Because of limited production, original 4-4-2 trim is difficult to find.

SUMMARY

One of the truly hot collectible Oldsmobiles: The only reason I won't risk five stars on the coupe is because I think it may have reached its crest of popularity. A small supply, owing to very low production, means that this muscle Olds will remain expensive, and that the value of good ones will continue to rise.

PRODUCTION	*1964*	*1965*
	2,999	unknown

1964-65 Cutlass 4-4-2

ENGINE
Type . . . . 90-deg V-8, water-cooled, cast-iron block and heads
Bore x stroke . . . . 3.94x3.38 in. (1964), 4.00x3.98 in. (1965)
Displacement . . . . 330 ci (1964), 400 ci (1965)
Valve operation . . . . hydraulic
Compression ratio 10.25:1
Carburetion . . . . downdraft 4-bbl
Bhp . . . . 290 gross at 5200 rpm (1964), 345 at 4800 (1965)
CHASSIS & DRIVETRAIN
Transmission . . . . 4-spd manual
Rear axle ratio . . . . 3.55:1, 3.23:1 (later with automatic)
Front suspension . . . . independent, heavy-duty coil springs, tube shocks
Rear suspension . . link-type, live axle, coil springs, tube shocks
GENERAL
Wheelbase . . . . 115 in.
Overall length . . . . 203.0 in. (1964), 204.4 in. (1965)
Track . . . . 58 in.
Tire size 7.75x14
Weight . . . . 3,200 lb
PERFORMANCE
Acceleration . . . . 0-60: 7.5 sec
Top speed . . . . 125 mph
Fuel mileage . . . . 10-14 mpg

Chapter 20

Toronado
1966-67

HISTORY

It took a Cord owner to point this out, but there was a lot of the old Cord 810/812 in the Toronado. Consider that front-wheel drive, combined with the latter's front end, hidden headlamps and big slotted wheels. It's doubtful the Toronado will ever reach the classic heights of the Cord, however.

There were a lot more Tornados, for one thing. But it is certain that the 1966-67 models are among the most desirable Oldsmobiles ever built.

Project engineer Andy Watt's goal was to combine traditional American big-car power with outstanding handling and traction. Toronado's 425 ci V-8 was shared with

This magnificent 1966 Toronado is owned by Dave and Pat Kennedy. Photography by Bud Juneau.

conventional full-size Olds models, but was teamed with a new "two-piece" transmission.

The torque converter was mounted behind the engine, the gearbox was located remotely under the left cylinder bank, and both were connected by a chain drive and sprocket. The virtually unbreakable yet flexible chain drive was developed to save weight and cut costs. It also resulted in a very compact engine/drivetrain package, and a front/rear weight distribution of 54/46—remarkable for a front-wheel-drive car.

Toronado styling was as sophisticated as its mechanicals. The C-pillars fell gently from the roof, there was no obvious beltline aft of the rear windows and the roofline flowed downward smoothly, into a rakish fastback. The curved fuselage was set off by boldly flared wheel arches. The front and rear were clean and wrapped tightly underneath, as were the sides.

The public responded enthusiastically, and over 40,000 Toronados were sold in the first model year. However, this was only an initial spurt, and sales were half that high in 1967. Gradually they worked their way back, and in banner year 1972, Oldsmobile produced nearly 50,000.

IDENTIFICATION

1966: Big, flared wheel arches connected by lower body crease mark the early Toronados. The '66 model's wide, horizontal bar grille, hidden headlamps and big, ventilated wheels strongly invoke the Cord image.

1967: A new, egg-crate grille; headlamp covers now flush with the hood.

PERFORMANCE AND UTILITY

One of the great American road cars, the Toronado runs effortlessly at 100 mph and can do 135 when pressed, even with a standard axle ratio and automatic transmission. Understeer is present, as in all front-wheel-drive cars, but is well controlled and never excessive. Rear compartment room is restricted and visibility out the rear quarters is not good, nor is gas mileage. (But who cares, if you're driving one?)

PROBLEM AREAS

For such a revolutionary new design, the first Toronado was remarkably free of bugs, partly because it was built on exclusive, slower-moving assembly lines. The '66s do chew up tires, but tire technology has improved over the years. Doors were heavy to open and close—a built-in assist arrived on 1967 and later models.

The engine/drivetrain was strong, but the combination of Quadrajet carb and high

Kamm-back tail has wall-to-wall lights and large bumper pan which dirties easily because of exhaust placement, and may be impossible to restore.

The Cord 810 inspired Olds stylists when Lansing revived the Cord concept of a big, front-wheel-drive grand tourer. Unlike Cord, headlamp doors popped up electrically.

underhood temperatures caused a rash of engine fires. Carbs should be checked regularly. Exhaust systems wear out quickly and are expensive to replace. Bodies were not rust-prone, but bumpers were. Most early Toronados show bumper dings and rust, and replacement or rechroming is costly.

SUMMARY AND PROSPECTS

Clearly the outstanding Oldsmobile model of the 1960s, and very possibly the best Olds of all time, the Toronado was distinct and unimitated—especially in its original, clean form of 1966-67. Given these considerations, fine examples are underpriced—they can still be found for under $10,000. But like all cars of this class, they change hands rarely, and usually between friends. Ten years from now it is fairly safe to predict price tags in the $25,000 range or more. At present, a "best buy."

PRODUCTION	1966	1967
standard	6,333	1,770
deluxe	34,630	20,020

1966-67 Toronado

ENGINE

Type	90-deg V-8, water-cooled, cast-iron block and heads
Bore x stroke	4.13x3.98 in.
Displacement	425 ci
Valve operation	hydraulic
Compression ratio	10.5:1
Bhp	385 gross at 4800 rpm

CHASSIS & DRIVETRAIN

Transmission	Turbo Hydra-matic
Axle ratio	3.21:1
Front suspension	independent torsion bar
Rear suspension	dead axle, longitudinal leaf springs, angled shocks

GENERAL

Wheelbase	119 in.
Overall length	211 in.
Track	63.5 in. front, 63.0 in. rear
Tire size	8.85x15
Weight	4,310-4,366 lb

PERFORMANCE

Acceleration	0-60: 8.5 sec
Top speed	135 mph
Fuel mileage	10-14 mpg

Toronado badges are more easily obtainable than some other trim bits.

Back-end hardware is scarce and expensive; the quarter panels are also subject to rust.

Dashboard was not a piece of inspired design, but there were genuine needle gauges, and controls were all grouped within easy reach of the driver.

Very Cord-like, slotted wheels help ventilate the big drums underneath, which are themselves finned.

Some Toronado connoisseurs feel the car lost its Cord-like distinction in 1967, when the horizontal bar grille was dropped in favor of an egg-crate; side styling was little changed except for wheels. Headlamp covers were now flush with hoodline.

Cutlass 4-4-2
1966-67

★★★

HISTORY

Continuation of the successful high-performance package introduced in 1964, the 4-4-2 had its own grillework and taillights, along with a few bits of special ornamentation, to set it off from the standard Cutlass. Functional hood louvers were fitted to the 1967 models. An anomaly, considering the 4-4-2 name, was the 1966 option of three two-barrel carburetors in place of the usual four-barrel, which delivered another 10 bhp.

Distinctive styling on the 1966 4-4-2 included special grille and taillamps, recessed front fender scoops, plain hood and deck lid and special badges. Quadrajet-equipped 400 V-8 provided lots of power, tri-carb option gave more.

The 4-4-2 package was available for 1966 in no fewer than five body styles: standard and sport coupe, standard and deluxe Holiday hardtop, and convertible. But this lineup shrank in 1967. The 4-4-2's GM B-body was in its last years then, and would be replaced by a new design with a shorter coupe wheelbase in 1968.

The cars were just as fast as ever, though the market for factory hot rods had peaked by then. Olds added many voluntary safety features in 1967, including dual master cylinder, hazard flashers, shoulder belts, padded steering wheel and glareproof rearview mirror.

IDENTIFICATION

1966: Blacked-out grille and tail panel, 4-4-2 badges, scoops on front fenders behind wheel arches.

1967: Fender scoops eliminated, hood louvers and paint striping added. Both models carried redline tires as standard equipment.

PERFORMANCE AND UTILITY

The archetypal muscle cars, 4-4-2s were cat-quick off the line and capable of a terrific turn of speed, underbraked (front discs improved this in 1967) and fairly skittish handlers on twisty roads, especially in the rain. There was not much room in the back, and visibility was only mediocre. Premium fuel was and is required.

PROBLEM AREAS

Again, a reliable drivetrain, mechanical layout and body make this a good model for restorers. However, some rust problems occur, even under vinyl tops and around rear windows. Competition for NOS and even good used parts is tremendous. During this era, Olds began to code its performance parts and packages with a W. Finding these parts is almost impossible, and when they are discovered, prices will be high. (See also Chapter 19.)

Last year for the old body was 1967. Alloy-style wheels were an improvement. The '67 also had dual master cylinder, hazard flashers, shoulder belts, padded steering wheel and glare-proof rearview mirror.

SUMMARY AND PROSPECTS

From the golden years of the factory-built street racers, 4-4-2s are strong on today's market and will continue to be good investments, especially the convertibles. As always with relatively recent cars, collectors should look for clean, low-mileage originals in lieu of "restorable" examples, because the more recent a car, the harder it will be to restore, owing to mounting technical complexity.

PRODUCTION	1966	1967
coupe	1,430*	—
hardtop	3,827*	—
sport coupe	3,937*	4,282
Holiday hardtop	10,043*	24,183
convertible	2,750*	5,142

Production figures estimated from a combined total of 21,997 stated by Olds Division.

1966-67 Cutlass 4-4-2

ENGINE
Type .... 90-deg V-8, water-cooled, cast-iron block and heads
Bore x stroke .... 4.00x3.98 in.
Displacement .... 400 ci
Valve operation .... hydraulic
Compression ratio 10.5:1
Carburetion ..... downdraft; 4-bbl (std), three 2-bbl (opt 1966)
Bhp .... 350 gross at 5000 rpm, 360 at 5000 (tri-carb)

CHASSIS & DRIVETRAIN
Transmission .... 4-spd, automatic opt
Rear axle ratio .... 3.08:1 std
Front suspension ...... independent, coil springs, tube shocks
Rear suspension .... live axle, 4-link, coil springs, tube shocks

GENERAL
Wheelbase .... 115 in.
Overall length .... 204.2 in.
Track .... 58 in. front, 59 in. rear
Tire size 7.75x14
Weight .... 2,600 lb (coupe), 3,200 lb (convertible)

PERFORMANCE
Acceleration .... 0-60: 7.5 sec
Top speed .... 125 mph
Fuel mileage .... 10-14 mpg

With fender scoops eliminated, '67 model lost some identity, which Olds tried to restore with paint striping on front fenders and doors. Red-line tires were stock in both years and should be added by owners for authenticity.

Chapter 22

Hurst/Olds
1968-69, 1972

★★★★

HISTORY

The first Hurst/Olds was a custom, designed for George Hurst of the famous shifter company by Doc Watson, the performance tuner. Olds expressed interest, so Hurst and Lansing competition supplier John Demmer got together to conjure up a dealer package. This included a 390 bhp 455 with special cam, crankshaft and heads, Turbo Hydra-matic with the inevitable Hurst shifter, forced-air induction, Goodyear G70 Polyglas tires, a performance axle

Smooth deck had black finish on the '68 model. Big, slotted wheels contributed to brake cooling. Note the jumbo dual exhausts poking out from the bumper pan.

ratio and special trim and badging.

Special paint jobs and striping were typical of Hurst/Olds cars. Assembly was by Oldsmobile but some final tweaking, polishing and a few small components were put on at Demmer Engineering, which had an assembly area for the project.

After a two-year hiatus (1970 and 1971), the Hurst/Olds made its second appearance as a trim option based on the Cutlass Su-

Olds Division comparison drawings of the original 1968 and 1969 Hurst/Olds show what a difference a hood scoop and spoiler can make on essentially the same body.

preme hardtops and convertibles. This time it used the 455 engine, suitably modified and with dual exhausts, a handling suspension, Hurst dual gate shifter and special paint job with Hurst badging.

Hurst/Olds options were novel, including a digital performance computer, a burglar alarm, an electric sunroof and the W-30 performance package.

The model vanished again in 1973, but would make more comebacks (see Chapters 27 and 28).

IDENTIFICATION

1968: Special silver paint with two gloss-black stripes on hood, atop fenders and along the beltline.

1969: Special gold and white paint job, large hood scoop and rear deck spoiler.

1972: Twin hood scoops, white paint with gold fender-outline stripes and gold bands on hood behind scoops.

PROBLEM AREAS

Unlike some Olds muscle cars, many Hurst/Olds wound up in the hands of adult owners who lavished them with care and kept to the maintenance schedule. Parts that interchange with the garden-variety F-85/Cutlass are relatively easy to find.

The '68 silver paint has a tendency to fade over the years, and stripes on all models can cause restoration nightmares. Even with reproduction suppliers in the picture, re-striping a Hurst/Olds is quite a project. Blending new stripes with old is difficult, too.

Special gold and white paint job, along with twin-snorkel scoop and deck spoiler, distin-guished the 1969 model. Divided grille was common to all Oldsmobiles that year.

Small interior or exterior trim pieces exclusive to the Hurst/Olds are rare.

SUMMARY AND PROSPECTS

A legendary muscle car, possibly destined for the heights among collectible Oldsmobiles, but it's too early to make predictions. Whether or not the current boom in muscle cars is permanent has yet to be determined, so I'll give it four stars for now. Undoubtedly, good examples of the Hurst/Olds will always be sought after. This is one late-model worth a restoration, if you can find or replicate the oddball parts.

PRODUCTION	1968*	1969	1972
Holiday hardtop	451	906	—
sport coupe	64	—	499
convertible	—	—	130

155 cars were fitted with air-conditioning in 1968.

1968-69, 1972 Hurst/Olds

ENGINE
Type . . . . 90-deg V-8, water-cooled, cast-iron block and heads
Bore x stroke . . . . 4.13x4.25 in.
Displacement . . . . 455 ci
Valve operation . . . . hydraulic
Compression ratio 10.25:1 (1968-69), 8.5:1 (1972)
Carburetion . . . . downdraft 4-bbl
Bhp . . . . . 390 gross at 5000 rpm (1968-69), 300 net at 4200 rpm (1972)

CHASSIS & DRIVETRAIN
Transmission . . . . . . Modified Turbo Hydra-matic, Hurst shifter
Rear axle ratio 3.23:1
Front suspension . . . . . . independent, coil springs, tube shocks
Rear suspension . . link-type, live axle, coil springs, tube shocks

GENERAL
Wheelbase . . . . 112 in.
Overall length . . . . 202 in. (1968-69), 204 in. (1972)
Track . . . . 59 in.
Tire size G70x14
Weight . . . . approx. 3,400 lb (coupe), 3,500 lb (convertible)

PERFORMANCE
Acceleration . . . . 0-60: 6-7 sec
Top speed . . . . 130 mph
Fuel mileage . . . . 8-12 mpg

Hurst reappeared on 1972 Cutlass Supreme base as trim option, using modified 455 engine, special paint job and badging. Performance computer, burglar alarm and electric sunroof were options.

Chapter 23

Toronado
1968-70

HISTORY

Continuation of the by then widely accepted front-wheel-drive Oldsmobile personal luxury car, which sold steadily—possibly because GM had wisely brought in the front-wheel-drive Cadillac Eldorado at a much higher price.

But the change-it-regardless people were having their way again, and the front end was hammed up with a massive, combination bumper-grille, wrapped around at the sides with all the panache of a 1949 Frazer. This ugly puss was continued in '69, but a decent facelift without the huge chrome shell arrived in '70. Unfortunately, the '70 also lost the unique, prominent wheel arches, so these Toronados have less-distinct styling personalities than their 1966-67 progenitors.

All 1968-70s, however, had the new, smooth and powerful 455 V-8, with a whopping 375 bhp standard and 400 optional, the

For 1969, the Toronado was 3½ inches longer, and crisper at the rear, though much less distinctive. Electrically heated window and power-ful 455 V-8, with a defogging system, was introduced as an option this year. Vinyl roof covering interferes with clean design on this one.

Huge bumper-grille combination changed the
look of the Toronado for 1968, many thought
for the worst. But the new 455 V-8 gave 375 to
400 hp and commensurately better performance,
so there was a consolation.

latter through a high-lift camshaft and cold-air induction. This gave the Toronado at least as much urge as before, as well as a slightly greater fuel thirst.

IDENTIFICATION

1968: Heavy chrome bumper-grille wrapped at corners, cam-back rear end styling. Olds emblem on fuel filler panel.

1969: Bumper-grille continued, but creased rear fenders and more rounded deck lid replaced 1968 rear end styling; no emblem on fuel filler panel.

1970: Wrapped bumper-grille eliminated in favor of nerf-like vertical bars in leading edges of front fenders, quad headlamps deeply inset in finer mesh grille, and slotted parking lights between grille and fender edges. Prominent wheel arches of all previous Toronados eliminated.

PROBLEM AREAS

Even when new, the Toronado was an expensive car to work on. Relatively common parts are expensive to replace.

Rust can pop up in lower body areas and under vinyl tops. Hidden headlamps look great, but as these cars age they tend to fail, and troubleshooting them is tricky. (See also Chapter 20.)

PERFORMANCE AND UTILITY

As fast and tractable as ever, thanks to the new 455 V-8, and slightly more horsepower to compensate for increasing weight. Usual cramped space for rear seat passengers, with all kinds of room up front. Inevitably thirsty, though able to accept lower-octane fuel than previous models, which is critical in some locations.

SUMMARY AND PROSPECTS

In various small ways, the 1968-70 generation of Toronados lacks the flavor of the 1966-67 originals, and an awareness of this among astute collectors has shown up in values. Car for car, a good 1968-70 Toronado will cost perhaps thirty to forty percent less than a good '66, with the transition '67 model somewhere between the two. The gap will probably widen in coming years.

Particularly desirable is the 1970 GT package, with special trim and higher performance. It is rare, however, and collectors are aware of it.

PRODUCTION	1968	1969	1970
hardtop	3,957	3,421	2,351
custom hardtop	22,497	25,073	23,082

1968-70 Toronado

ENGINE
Type .... 90-deg V-8, water-cooled, cast-iron block and heads
Bore x stroke .... 4.13x4.25 in.
Displacement .... 455 ci
Valve operation .... hydraulic
Compression ratio 10.25:1
Bhp .... 375 gross at 4600 rpm (std), 400 gross at 4800 rpm (opt 1968-69), 400 gross at 4000 rpm (1970)

CHASSIS & DRIVETRAIN
Transmission .... Turbo Hydra-matic
Rear axle ratio 3.08:1 (1968), 3.07:1 (1969-70)
Front suspension .... torsion bar
Rear suspension .... dead axle, longitudinal leaf springs, angled shocks

GENERAL
Wheelbase .... 119 in.
Overall length .... 211.4 in. (1968), 214.8 in. (1969), 214.3 in. (1970)
Track .... 63.5 in. front, 63 in. rear
Tire size 8.85x14 (1968), 8.85x15 (1969), J78x15 (1970)
Weight .... 4,316-4,386 lb

PERFORMANCE
Acceleration .... 0-60: 9.0 sec
Top speed .... 130 mph
Fuel mileage .... 10-14 mpg

Big changes in 1970: Wheel arches disappeared, grille was entirely revised and much busier with exposed headlights for the first time. For these reasons the '70 is not as admired among collectors as the earlier models.

Chapter 24

4-4-2
1968-71

★★★	convertibles
★★	coupes

HISTORY

Redesigned along with all the GM B-bodies in 1968, the 4-4-2 then hit its peak years of development, as a separate Olds series rather than a trim package of the Cutlass line. Dealers ordered model number 344, which in all four years brought a convertible, though the traditional pillarless hardtop was dropped in 1971.

A Hurst three-speed, the 400/455 V-8s, dual exhausts and wide oval tires were legendary 4-4-2 hallmarks. They were accompanied by cold-air induction, power front disc brakes, transistorized ignition, limited-slip differential, a multitude of needle gauges, and special stripping and badging.

Optionally in 1969, Olds offered the ex-

A 1968 4-4-2 owned by Michael Morocco is an excellent example of the breed in its first year as a separate Oldsmobile series. This and subsequent photos of the '68 by Bud Juneau.

plosive W-30 package: air induction 400, 360 bhp and a range of rear axle ratios all the way to 4.66:1. The same package in 1970 included a 370 hp 455 engine, which probably produced more like 400 bhp.

Sales of muscle cars were well down then, as the public tired of stump-pulling performance, and soldiers drafted for Vietnam eliminated a large number of potential customers. The 4-4-2 had garnered 33,000 sales in the '68 model year; for 1971, its last year as a separate series, it claimed only 7,500. After '71, it reverted to an option, available on selected Cutlass models.

IDENTIFICATION

1968: Blacked-out grille with "442" badge centered, "442" and Olds rocket badge on deck. Striping package (when applied) was

Fender badges repeated the message, which seems blatant enough already.

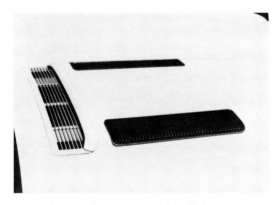

Cold-air induction was available via large breathing slot on the hood, but other scoops are not what they seem.

vertical on front fenders.

1969: Divided grille with "442" on central steel panel; rocket badge dropped from deck. Marker lights on fenders were amber.

1970: Vertical pattern grille was not black; twin hood scoops.

1971: Grille blacked out again with "442" on driver's side, rocket badge in grille panel. Round parking lamps took the place of oblong versions.

PERFORMANCE AND UTILITY

Traditional 4-4-2 performance is available up through the 1970 model. The '71 was considerably slower and, withal, not that exciting. Usual 4-4-2 utility problems of limited space in back and in trunk. The cars tend to require premium gas, and are of course very thirsty.

PROBLEM AREAS

These big-block-powered cars gave good engine/drivetrain service, and there is very good body/mechanical interchangeability with other Cutlass models, even other years. Underhood problems were few on well-maintained cars, but infrequent oil changes did cause rocker arm problems and noisy lifters.

Careful scrutiny is nevertheless important before your purchase. Many were flogged from the day they smoked their

Heavy-duty wheels were a part of the 4-4-2 package in 1968, with 14 in. Super Stock wheels optional. The same package in 1970 included a 370 hp 455 engine, which probably produced nearer to 400 bhp.

tires off the dealer lot. Rust occurs in the rocker and quarter panel areas, on bumpers and around the front and rear glass.

These are already popular collectibles. If you doubt that, try trekking around Carlisle looking for 1968-71 4-4-2 goodies. W-performance items like ram-air hood, air-induction parts and rear spoilers are all but extinct as NOS or used parts.

SUMMARY AND PROSPECTS

The relative mediocrity of the '71's performance may be balanced valuewise by its scarcity. Overall, however, these later 4-4-2s will rank in value according to their years of manufacture, with the '68s and '69s clearly preferable, and convertibles of all years more desirable than coupes. Not as rapid in appreciation as earlier muscle cars, and probably good buys at present, but look for examples that require little rebuilding or bodywork.

1968-71 4-4-2, 1972 4-4-2 W-30	
ENGINE	
Type	90-deg V-8, water-cooled, cast-iron block and heads
Bore x stroke	4.00x3.98 in. (1968-69), 4.13x4.25 in. (1970-72)
Displacement	400 ci (1968-69), 455 ci (1970-72)
Valve operation	hydraulic
Compression ratio	10.5:1 (1968-70), 8.5:1 (1971-72)
Carburetion	downdraft 4-bbl
Bhp	350 gross at 4800 rpm std, 360 at 5400 opt (1968-69); 365 gross at 4000 rpm std, 370 gross at 5200 opt (1970); 350 net at 4200 rpm (1971); 300 net at 4200 rpm (1972)
CHASSIS & DRIVETRAIN	
Transmission	4-spd, Hydra-matic opt
Rear axle ratio	2.78:1 to 3.23:1
Front suspension	independent, coil springs, tube shocks
Rear suspension	live axle, coil springs, tube shocks
GENERAL	
Wheelbase	112 in.
Overall length	202.0 to 203.5 in. approx
Track	59 in.
Tire size	G70x14
Weight	3,100 lb (1968-69 coupes), 3,400 lb (all 1970-72)
PERFORMANCE	
Acceleration	0-60: 8-9 sec (1968-71), 10-11 sec (1972)
Top speed	120 mph (1968-71), 105 mph (1972)
Fuel mileage	10-13 mpg

Blacked-out grille with central badge and big numerals on front fenders easily identifies Olds' muscle car. Trim parts and striping are now almost impossible to find among new-old-stock.

PRODUCTION	1968	1969	1970	1971
convertible	5,142	4,295	2,933	1,304
sport coupe	4,282	2,475	1,688	6,285
hardtop	24,183	19,587	14,709	—

The 1969 model was cleaned up, bereft of dummy hood scoops, replaced by rally paint scheme which was repeated on front fenders. Forced-air induction remained optional.

The potent W-30 engine is part of this hot 1970
4-4-2 package owned by Dave Cobble II. This
and subsequent photos by Bud Juneau.

Interior was not helped by obviously fake woodgraining, but was notably clean, with prominent
Hurst shifter.

Stylists went back to the blatant look in 1969, with huge hood scoops painted black, and bold vertical grille slots.

The sign of power: Never again would Oldsmobile build a rocket quite like this 1970 model.

Taillights and surrounding chrome are subject to discoloration over the course of time, from the W-30's huge dual exhaust outlets.

By far the most common model was the hardtop, but you would look long and hard to find a more desirable 4-4-2 than Cobble's outstanding W-30. Its '71 successor was toned down.

The 1970 W-30 option package included PK5, 670x14 in. wide-oval tires, and these or comparable tires should be sought out by today's owners.

Hood scoops were functional, as were the twist-type hood hold-down locks.

Best thing the '71 model has going for it is scarcity. This convertible is one of only 1,304 examples, the lowest production run among the cars in this chapter.

Streamlined racing-type rearview mirrors were interior-adjustable, and are hard to replace authentically.

Chapter 25

Cutlass Rallye 350

1970

★★★

HISTORY

An interesting substitute for the Hurst/ Olds (which turned up missing this year), the Rallye 350 included the following: 350 high-compression four-barrel V-8, fiberglass forced-air hood intake, custom sport steering wheel, styled sport outside rearview mirrors, deck-lid spoiler, rally suspension and dual exhaust system. Also provided was the W-45 appearance package: Sebring yellow paint with black and orange decals for hood, fender peaks and rear-body silhouette; urethane-coated Sebring yellow bumpers; blacked-out grille; custom-painted Super Stock II wheels with G70×14 inch wide-oval blackwall tires; and a bold "Rallye

A beautiful Rallye 350 owned by Domenic and Ellen Santucci. Photographs of this car by Bud Juneau.

350" decal. (Optional PK5 or PX8 tires could be ordered.)

It was an alluring car if you went for that kind of thing. The '70s, incidentally, were the first new Olds models introduced by General Manager John Beltz, a popular young engineer who replaced Harold Metzel after Metzel's retirement in April 1969. Beltz said he expected people to be impressed with the Rallye 350's looks, but that "we believe they will be even more impressed when they drive it." The times were not right for such a package, however, and fewer than 4,000 were sold.

IDENTIFICATION

Unmistakable Sebring yellow body with black and orange decals and a "Rallye 350" decal, rear deck spoiler and blacked-out grille.

PERFORMANCE AND UTILITY

The four-barrel 350 delivered 310 to 325 gross bhp, which gave very impressive acceleration. The usual problems of GM intermediate coupes were present, including poor visibility, limited space in the rear seat and trunk and mediocre assembly quality.

PROBLEM AREAS

The obvious problems exist here for the collector/restorer. Mechanical and sheet metal interchangeability with other Cutlass and F-85 models is good, but like its cousin the Hurst/Olds, the Rallye 350 used decals that are now almost nonexistent. And the originals did not fare well, except under ideal storage conditions. However, the Rallye 350 Chapter of the Oldsmobile Club of America has a decal source, and this has helped get some examples of this model back in circulation.

Being a single-year offering makes other Rallye 350 trim items scarce. The yellow-coated bumpers are difficult to repair and replacements are very costly.

SUMMARY AND PROSPECTS

The Rallye 350 was rare in its day and is extremely scarce now, though not as uncommon as the Hurst/Olds. It has enjoyed a strong collector demand for the last six or eight years, and is destined to be quite a valuable model in the future. How valuable depends as usual on the condition of the individual car. Once again, my perennial reminder to anyone thinking about buying such a relatively modern car: Get one in as good original condition as possible. In the Rallye's case, you may not have many alternatives to choose from. But be patient, and wait for a good one to come along.

Standard color was Sebring yellow, repeated in poly bumpers, with orange and black decals.

G70x14 wide-oval blackwalls were mounted on Sebring yellow slotted wheels.

1970 Cutlass S Rallye 350

ENGINE

Type . . . . 90-deg V-8, water-cooled, cast-iron block and heads
Bore x stroke . . . . 4.06x3.38 in.
Displacement . . . . 350 ci
Valve operation . . . . hydraulic
Compression ratio . . . . 9.0:1 (std), 10.25:1 & 10.5:1 (opt)
Carburetion . . . . downdraft 2-bbl (std), 4-bbl (opt)
Bhp . . . . . 250 gross at 4400 rpm (std), 310 gross at 4800 rpm &
   325 gross at 5400 rpm (opt)

CHASSIS & DRIVETRAIN

Transmission . . . . 3-spd, 4-spd, Hydra-matic
Rear axle ratio . . . . 3.08:1 to 3.23:1
Front suspension . . . . . . independent, coil springs, tube shocks
Rear suspension . . . . live axle, coil springs, tube shocks

GENERAL

Wheelbase . . . . 112 in.
Overall length . . . . 203 in.
Track . . . . 59 in.
Tire size G70x14
Weight . . . . 3,450 lb

PERFORMANCE

Acceleration . . . . 0-60: 7-8 sec (4-bbl), 10-11 sec (2-bbl)
Top speed . . . . 100-110 mph
Fuel mileage . . . . 12-18 mpg

PRODUCTION

Oldsmobile built 3,547 units in the sport coupe and Holiday coupe bodies, each with bench or bucket seats. A breakdown is not available, but overall, Cutlass S Holidays outsold sport coupes eight to one. Since most Rallye 350 buyers wanted buckets, you can assume that a bucket-seat Holiday coupe is the most common variation, while a bench-seat standard coupe is the scarcest (but not necessarily the most desirable— who wants bench seats in a car like this?).

Bold announcement decals emblazoned the rear fenders; airfoil spoiler on deck was standard equipment, as were orange and black detail trim. Note body-colored polyurethane bumpers; these hold up well and seldom need serious attention.

By now familiar, the Olds dual-snorkel hood scoops, done up in flashy black with orange trim on the 350.

The Rallye 350 was an unmistakable car, and
with fewer than 4,000 built, it stands to remain
highly collectible among muscle Oldsmobiles.

Chapter 26

98 Regency 75th Anniversary Edition

1972

★★

HISTORY

Oldsmobile was the first company to turn seventy-five years old, and in recognition of the milestone, a commemorative edition of the 98 Regency four-door hardtop was released in the spring of 1972. In keeping with then-current trends, the largest Olds was longer and lower, but notably clean of nonfunctional decoration. The divided grille and rectangular-set quad headlamps had come in the year before.

The windshield angle was very rakish, while the side glass curved to continue the sheet metal contour. Although the four-door hardtop's popularity was then on the wane, it would remain available in the 98 series until the downsizing program of 1977.

The 75th Anniversary Edition included a velour interior in black or gold, a Tiffany

Factory photo of the Regency summarizes its combination of immense size and luxury. Paint was "Anniversary gold metallic," and interior featured a Tiffany clock. A peripheral collect-ible, but of some historic interest, not only as an Olds commemorative edition but as one of the last dinosaurs.

clock, Anniversary gold metallic paint and a special key with a sterling silver key ring.

IDENTIFICATION

Unique gold paint with black or gold quilted velour interior and Tiffany clock.

PERFORMANCE AND UTILITY

A slow and clumsy full-size six-passenger land yacht, with all that infers about smooth riding comfort and luxury combined with sloppy handling and fuel thirst. Notably well assembled, according to the reviews of contemporary road testers. The 455 V-8, however, was no longer really appropriate, and was detuned considerably in 1972, though not as much as it was later.

PROBLEM AREAS

A fairly reliable model, for which mechanical and body parts are in good supply and inexpensive. As with a number of Oldsmobiles finished in metallic paint, fading of the Regency gold was a common problem. Interior fabrics were also vulnerable, and replacement fabric is tough to find.

SUMMARY AND PROSPECTS

A peripheral collector car whose main qualification is that it commemorated an important date in history. In itself, it is a reminder of the onetime standard of the typical American car, a standard that will never exist again. For collectors of such social artifacts, this combination of character may be attractive, but its value cannot be expected to shoot upward very rapidly.

PRODUCTION
Several thousand.

1972 98 Regency 75th Anniversary Edition

ENGINE
Type	90-deg V-8, water-cooled, cast-iron block and heads
Bore x stroke	4.13x4.25 in.
Displacement	455 ci
Valve operation	hydraulic
Compression ratio	8.5:1
Carburetion	downdraft 4-bbl
Bhp	225 net at 3600 rpm

CHASSIS & DRIVETRAIN
Transmission	Turbo Hydra-matic
Rear axle ratio	2.73:1
Front suspension	independent, coil springs, tube shocks
Rear suspension	live axle, coil springs, tube shocks

GENERAL
Wheelbase	127 in.
Overall length	227.2 in.
Track	63.6 in.
Tire size	J78-15
Weight	4,567 lb

PERFORMANCE
Acceleration	0-60: 14 sec
Top speed	90-95 mph
Fuel mileage	12-16 mpg

Chapter 27

Hurst/Olds
1974-75

HISTORY

Third revival of the Hurst package in the relatively peace-loving, citizen's pack, as required by the politicians a decade-plus ago. A pair of these with rakish roll bars comprised the C-pillars, the roof between them and the windshield header having been removed (and the chassis beefed-up to stand the flex). Road-going Hurst/Olds used the "colonnade" coupe styling then prevalent on the Cutlass S series; Indy

Pace Car replicar lettering and striping was optional.

Born again in 1975, the model came back as a demi-convertible with a T-roof based on the 1974 Indy Pace Car, better braced thanks to a connecting panel between the C- and A-pillars. The Hurst Hatch featured removable, tinted laminated glass panels which were placed in a special case in the trunk. Paint was black or white with gold racing stripes.

IDENTIFICATION

1974: Usual Hurst insignias inside and out, alloy road wheels, dark banded C-pillar contrasting with white paint job.

1975: Black or white with Hurst/Olds emblems on rear (vinyl-padded) roof quarters and louvers on center of hood. "W-30" or "W-31" lettering on front fenders.

PERFORMANCE AND UTILITY

Fitted with either the 350 or optional 455 V-8, the Hurst/Olds was as quick as an Olds got in those years. Styling was clean and functional, though the Indy Pace Car decals, optional on the '74, can hardly be called conservative. A better all-around car with the W-30 package, as the W-31s tended to be all-engine, but without the brakes and suspension to handle it. Hard suspension settings make Hurst/Olds relatively hard riders. Fit and finish quality were indifferent.

1974-75 Hurst/Olds

ENGINE
Type . . . . 90-deg V-8, water-cooled, cast-iron block and heads
Bore x stroke . . . . 4.06x3.38 in.
Displacement . . . . 355 ci
Valve operation . . . . hydraulic
Compression ratio 8.5:1
Carburetion . . . . downdraft 4-bbl
Bhp . . . . 200 net at 4200 rpm (1974); 180 net at 3800 rpm (1975)
CHASSIS & DRIVETRAIN
Transmission . . . . 3-spd, Turbo Hydra-matic
Rear axle ratio 2.73:1 (1974), 3.08:1 (1975)
Front suspension . . . . . . independent, coil springs, tube shocks
Rear suspension . . . . live axle, coil springs, tube shocks
GENERAL
Wheelbase . . . . 112 in.
Overall length . . . . 211.7 in.
Track . . . . 61.4 in.
Tire size F78-15 (1974), FR78-15 (1975)
Weight . . . . 3,980 lb (1974), 3,775 lb (1975)
PERFORMANCE
(With 350 engine)
Acceleration . . . . 0-60: 12 sec
Top speed . . . . 100 mph
Fuel mileage . . . . 14-18 mpg
Note: The 455 V-8 was optional; see Chapter 27 specifications

120

PROBLEM AREAS

As with all exclusive interior and exterior Hurst trim items, the search for replacement stock is difficult. The situation has been compounded by the fact that Cars and Concepts recently sold its Hurst Performance Division. Over the years Cars and Concepts had established a relationship with collectors, selling parts in inventory and even reproducing faster moving items. With the sale, it appears that this arrangement has ended. The Hurst/Olds Chapter of the Oldsmobile Club of America is some help in obtaining parts and working with those in the replacement arena. Some firms, however, have adopted the grab-the-cash philosophy and turned out shoddy, "outlaw"

Hurst/Olds bits and pieces. The moral: Know your parts source.

Stripes were a problem, as they always are. Originals are difficult to find. Reproductions can be had, but be sure they come from a reliable supplier. On the 1974 model, any decaling associated with the pace car replicas is doubly hard to find.

Rust can thrive in the lower underbody areas and under the special vinyl roof. Models equipped with the hatch roof were prone to water leakage, even when new.

SUMMARY AND PROSPECTS

Variable. Low production of the 1974 model means it is much scarcer, especially with the Indy Pace Car decals. On the other

Two views of the wild looking but in fact quite tame 1974 model in pace car replica form, using

GM's new colonnade styling with prominent, raked B-pillar. Only 380 were built.

hand, the Hurst Hatch of 1975 is an interesting feature that attracts many. All Hurst/Olds are in extreme demand today; whether they stay that way will depend on the permanence of the muscle car craze. But certainly, prices will not ever come down, and a super-clean example can already command five figures.

PRODUCTION	1974	1975
	380	2,535

Back again the next year, the Hurst/Olds featured a T-roof based on the Indy Pace Car from 1974, known as the Hurst Hatch, with removable tinted safety glass panels. Paint was black or white with gold stripes. Production was much higher at 2,535.

Chapter 28

Hurst/Olds

1983-84

★★?

HISTORY

A throwback to the glory days, this $2,000 trim package for the Cutlass Supreme Calais coupe comprised the optional five-liter (307 ci) four-barrel V-8, four-speed automatic with Hurst three-stick Lightning Rod shifter, firm suspension with air shocks and Goodyear Eagle GT tires.

This last-to-date Hurst/Olds permutation was no longer state of the art, lacking the traction of more modern front-wheel-drive intermediates—but somehow a front-wheel-drive Hurst/Olds isn't in character. The firm suspension made for better than average handling for a Cutlass, at the expense of ride.

IDENTIFICATION

Hurst/Olds badging inside and out, rear deck spoiler, styled steel wheels.

PERFORMANCE AND UTILITY

A muscled-up version of a popular model, noted for good driveability and a clean-shifting transmission, but not for fuel mileage. Off-the-line performance was good, considering. As usual with rear-wheel-drive General Motors intermediates, there was little room in the back, and a cramped trunk.

PROBLEM AREAS

Workmanship was generally good, but paint was rough in spots, trim did not line up properly on many cars and the interior, while well put together, could have done without the obviously fake wood trim. The 1978-81 Cutlass models were recalled to replace two rear suspension bolts likely to corrode and break, causing loss of control, but these problems have not seemed to affect later models. The cars are not old enough

Cutlass Supreme Calais provided the basis of the eighties Hurst/Olds revival, which used the best engine left (307 cubes) and four-speed automatic with Hurst Lightning Rod shifter plus tight suspension.

The new Hurst/Olds looked fairly hairy, and would do 0-60 in under nine seconds, which wasn't bad for the time. Olds claimed 17/27 mpg economy, but it was closer to the seventeen.

yet to indicate the extent of rust problems, but corrosion resistance has been good for earlier models. The parts supply is, of course, excellent, and will be for some years.

SUMMARY AND PROSPECTS

While it is much too soon to draw any conclusions, these eighties versions of the famous Hurst/Olds were certainly low-volume units with distinctive styling and all the right performance options. As such, they are bound to be considered by collectors—*if* collectors get interested in early-eighties intermediates in general. For now, predictions are difficult. Look on this one as a model of opportunity—if a really nice one comes along at a good price, you might be getting a sleeper.

PRODUCTION
Not known, but low.

1983-84 Hurst/Olds

ENGINE
Type	90-deg V-8, water-cooled, cast-iron block and heads
Bore x stroke	3.80x3.89 in.
Displacement	307 ci
Valve operation	hydraulic
Compression ratio	8.0:1
Carburetion	4-bbl downdraft
Bhp	140 net at 3600 rpm

CHASSIS & DRIVETRAIN
Transmission	3-spd, 4-spd, Hydra-matic
Rear axle ratio	2.14:1 (3-spd), 2.56:1 (4-spd)
Front suspension	independent, coil springs, tube shocks, swaybar
Rear suspension	rigid axle, 4-links, coil springs, optional swaybar

GENERAL
Wheelbase	108.1 in.
Overall length	200 in.
Track	58.5 in. front, 57.7 in. rear
Tire size	P195-75R14
Weight	3,204 lb

PERFORMANCE
Acceleration	0-60: 10 sec
Top speed	115 mph
Fuel mileage	14-20 mpg

Front and rear views of the 1984 version, which
were much the same, but the front is easily dis-
tinguishable by its vertical bar grille.

Chapter 29

Pace car replicas
1970-85

★★★★

HISTORY

Appropriately enough, though it was a different kind of racing, the Olds 88 paced the Indianapolis 500 in 1949, when it was wowing stock car fans on the NASCAR ovals. Oldsmobile was an official car at Indy in 1933 and the official Indy Pace Car in 1960, but pace car replicas for dealers to sell had not been thought of then. When the 1970 Indianapolis classic was again paced by a Cutlass 4-4-2, the Division immediately sent a handful of replicas into the field, and Olds tradition of replicating pace cars began.

IDENTIFICATION

1970: Cutlass 4-4-2 convertible with Goodyear white-letter tires and alloy road wheels. Also sold without pace car lettering.

1972: Cutlass Supreme Hurst/Olds convertible or hardtop with 455 ci engine, power front disc brakes, tuned suspension, dual exhausts, cold-air induction, Hunter

Oldsmobile had been at Indy in 1933, and had paced the 1949 and 1960 races, but replicas were not made until the fourth pace car, a 4-4-2 con- vertible, in 1970. This is the original, in pearl white with white top, black interior, and black and red striping.

shifter in center console, 3.23:1 rear axle ratio (very low for the time), twin sport mirrors and cameo white paint with gold striping. (See also Chapter 22.)

1974: Cutlass S colonnade hardtop (really a two-door sedan) with white paint job and gold striping, an extremely rare edition since only a fraction of the 380 Hurst/Olds were so equipped.

1977: Delta 88 Royale coupe with black and silver color scheme, special identification inside and out and Hurst shifter in central console.

1985: Calais 500 notchback coupe. Special metallic maroon paint with special leather interior. Exclusive interior and exterior trim, special handling package and V-6 power.

For 1972 there were Hurst/Olds convertibles and hardtops with the 455 engine. Cameo white with gold stripes was the color scheme.

PERFORMANCE AND UTILITY

Better-than-average performance and roadability than conventional versions of the same models, greater-than-average thirsts thanks to tuned engines, and harder riding than standard because of heavy-duty suspensions.

PROBLEM AREAS

Decals did not have staying power and may be partly destroyed. It is important to locate replacement decals, but these are in short supply. Badges and emblems are also hard to find. Metallic paint on the 1977 model tended to fade quickly.

PERFORMANCE AND UTILITY

Same as for high-output versions of standard models in these years.

PRODUCTION

Not broken out by Oldsmobile, but small.

The Cutlass S colonnade hardtop served as replica to this special official pace car, with B-pillar serving as a pseudo roll bar.

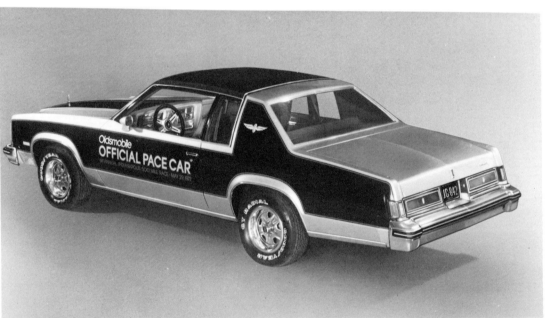

Delta 88 Royale coupes had distinctive silver and black paint jobs with Firethorn red interiors, GT radials mounted on red SS wheels, sport steering wheel, and so on.

James Garner drove the 1985 Indy 500 Pace Car, based on a Calais coupe, modified as a convertible. An example of its times, this pacer carried a 2.7 liter four-cylinder engine with 215 net horsepower.

Chapter 30

Show cars & specials
1954-69

HISTORY

Oldsmobile began exhibiting special show cars at the 1953 Motorama, and a few have survived. This chapter recounts each of these and provides identifying illustrations. The odds of finding one are infinitesimal . . . but it has happened before.

1953 Starfire

A low, sleek, turquoise prototype, this Corvette-like two-seater was named after Lockheed's F94B Starfire fighter. It prefigured several ideas that would reach production, although not necessarily by Oldsmobile: fiberglass bodywork, wraparound windshield, combination bumper-grille and bucket seats. Brake horsepower from the 308 V-8 was over 200, the first time this plateau had been reached.

1954 Cutlass

Another name that would see mass pro-

The Starfire with its namesake, the Air Force's Lockheed F94B fighter. Fiberglass bodywork was Corvette-like.

duction (and in a much bigger way than the Starfire), Cutlass was billed as "the ultimate in hardtops." Mounted on a 110 inch wheelbase, it featured fastback styling with a louvered backlight, the combination bumper-grille, swivel seats (much in advance of Chrysler's) and copper-toned glass for screening harsh light. The copper-metallic Cutlass was a predictive car in many ways; today's Saab 900 uses a copper-tinted glass, having determined that color to be the most effective.

1954 F-88

Corvette-inspired descendant of the '53 Starfire in brown metallic with pigskin upholstery, and powered by a 250 bhp 324 V-8, the F-88 featured cone-shaped clear plastic headlamp covers and a functional hood scoop. It was strictly a dream car, since the lukewarm sales of the Corvette pre-cluded any sports car cloning by the other GM divisions.

1955 Delta

A four-passenger close-coupled coupe just fifty-three inches high, mounted on a 120 inch wheelbase similar to that of the production 88. The Delta was designed to consider new materials and design features, many of which are taken for granted today: dual fuel tanks in the rear fenders, cast-aluminum wheels, anodized aluminum trim, a center console for radio controls and extra storage. Styling was strictly Harley Earl, very rounded with the dipped beltline that would permeate the GM line by 1957-58, and the car was two tones of metallic blue.

1956 Golden Rocket

A wild-looking bronze-metallic two-seat coupe was the most projectile-like Olds

The Cutlass, also a 1954 model, was heralded as "the ultimate in hardtops," rode a 110 inch wheelbase, and was distinctive through its backlight louvers, then a great novelty.

show car, and one of the quickest: Its 234 V-8 was tuned to produce 275 hp, which must have been impressive considering its curb weight of about 2,500 pounds. Like most of its predecessors, the Rocket had a fiberglass body. Roof panels rose, resembling Mercedes' gullwing-style, and the seats lifted and swiveled out to welcome the posterior when the doors were opened. Conventional bumpers were replaced by nerf-like built-in bumpers, and one of the first-known tilt steering wheels was in the cockpit.

1957 Mona Lisa

A 98 Holiday coupe finished in pearlescent tangerine with harmonizing upholstery, designed by Peggy Sauer of Olds Styling to express the feminine viewpoint. The Mona Lisa was counterpart to the more famous Dodge La Femme, neither of which would get much of a review today. Its purpose was to try new materials and gauge public reaction to them.

1957 Chanteuse

Another Peggy Sauer creation done in a high-luster violet with chartreuse interior accents, just as grim a combination as it

sounds. A violet umbrella was housed in a tube attached to the lower section of the right-hand door.

1957 F-88 Mark II

Updated version of the original, painted blue metallic and featuring design aspects of the forthcoming GM '58s, notably the Chevrolet Impala and Corvette. A big ovoid grille with vertical teeth and a nerf-type front bumper system distinguished this Harley Earl special.

1958 Carousel

A slightly modified Fiesta 98 wagon designed with children in mind, the metallic-blue Carousel combined fabric front seat with vinyl rear, and linoleum covering the rear cargo area. For child passengers, there was a magnetic car game on the back of the front seat, and elastic bands to organize the stowage of their gear. All hardware was removed from the inside rear door panels, and the rear doors could be released only from the instrument panel.

1959 F-88 Mark III

Bright red with a brushed aluminum retractable hardtop, this low, sleek two-seater

A Corvette in Olds livery, the F-88 mounted a big, central all-gauge cluster under its severely

wrapped windshield. It was powered by a 324 V-8.

was Earl's design swan song. Its 102 inch wheelbase carried a combination fiberglass and steel body, and it stood only forty-six inches high. Inside were bucket seats and aircraft-type instruments featuring rotating disc-type tachometer and speedometer, color-coded according to range. To obtain a very low hood, there was a special carburetor arrangement and an altered-from-stock crossflow aluminum radiator. The muffler/exhaust system was mounted *ahead* of the engine, exiting forward of the front wheels; an experimental Hydra-matic was mounted in the rear to improve weight distribution. Harley Earl drove the Mark III for a while during his retirement.

1962 X-215

A custom F-85 convertible, this Firefrost silver sportster had a fiberglass tonneau cover incorporating an airfoil section roll bar. Bucket seats, functional air scoops for brake cooling and a concave grille housing regular and long-range driving lights were other features.

1963 J-TR

Designed for the Chicago Automobile Show, this was a four-passenger F-85 convertible with custom interior and exterior colors and materials, cast-aluminum wheels, rectangular headlamps and louvered rocker panels housing stainless steel exhaust outlets.

1963 El Torero

Also at Chicago was this 98 convertible, resplendent in Firefrost gold paint, with Spanish-style brocaded interior featuring four individual bucket seats in red, black, gold and white.

1963 Custom Cutlass

A third Chicago car, mildly customized.

1964 4-4-2

Progenitor of the production 4-4-2 (400 bhp, four-barrel carb, twin exhausts) was a special Cutlass convertible with contoured "astronaut" bucket seats, a blacked-out grille, no bumper, dished chrome wheel covers and vivid red paint.

Delta, 1955, was a portent of the 1958 GM restyle. Painted duotone turquoise and deep blue, it was a hardtop with broad glass area and four bucket seats on a long wheelbase, close to that of the 88.

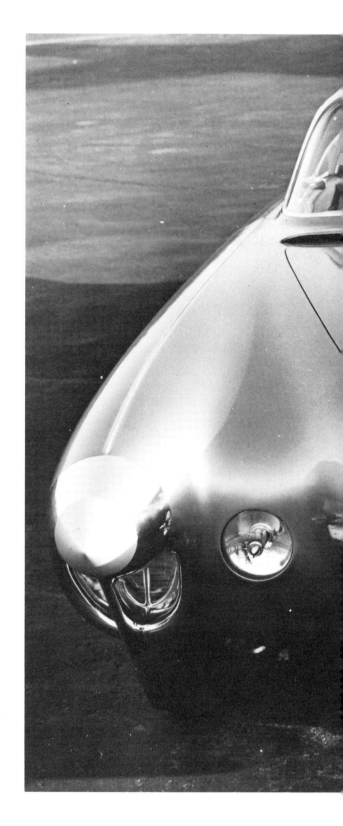

Phenomenal Golden Rocket had a backlight not unlike the famous Sting Ray Corvette coupe of seven years later. It belted out 275 hp and was said to be an honest road-going runner.

1964 Experimental 98
Painted Firefrost blue with a nautical-theme blue and white interior.

1966 Pasha
A 98 convertible for the down-home oil baron, with jeweled crest and script, fake mouton carpeting, suede and gold brocaded upholstery, cinnamon cashmere door panels, seats and convertible boot. The body color was Pasha Pearl lacquer.

1966 Gold Toronado
A showmobile painted gold metallic, with gold-plated hardware inside and out, widely displayed during the Toronado's maiden year but not, of course, available for sale.

1967 Toronado XX
In a novel design exercise, the Toronado's wheelbase was trimmed to 110 inches and considerable body was shaved off the front and rear ends, giving the XX a length of barely 200 inches. The result was a stunning, close-coupled, hunkered-down effect that was entirely complimentary. It's too bad such a short-wheelbase sports model didn't get into production.

1968 Toronado Granturismo
Successor to the Gold Toronado, with a blue-metallic paint job and special interior. Featured on this version were completely molded door panels (no metal garnishing), recessed door hardware, lots of protective safety padding, inertia reel shoulder harnesses and a roof console incorporating aircraft cockpit-like rocker switches for power windows, seat and interior lights. There were courtesy lamps in the doors to light the exit area; sequential flashers to warn approaching cars when the doors were open; reading lights; dome lights; and warning lamps for seat belts, low fuel, unlocked doors and emergency flasher. The Granturismo was a dual-edged production designed both to impress show-goers and to suggest Oldsmobile's concern with safety.

1968 Gold Toronado
New York show car finished throughout in metallic gold, based on standard Toronado.

1968 Mod Rod
A psychedelic-colored 4-4-2 shown at the

Fiberglass body featured rising roof panels (when doors were opened) and swivel seats. Huge Dagmar bumper guards protected rear end, with flip-down panel covering fuel filler.

Peggy Sauer of Oldsmobile Styling demonstrated neat built-in umbrella holder on the Chanteuse, a 1957 Motorama showmobile. Why haven't any manufacturers thought of that as a production car feature?

New York Automobile Show, trimmed in bright-yellow vinyl and carpeting.

1968 Cutlass S
Special show car painted Frost blue glaze.

1969 Apollo
A wild 4-4-2 convertible influenced by the space capsule from which it took its name, painted bright red with black accent striping and an interior of leather "couches," spaceship-like, with built-in head restraints, also done in red and black. Oldsmobile promoted the Apollo by explaining that the seat contours would help passengers withstand takeoff g-forces, and if only they could get the thing to fly. . . .

PERFORMANCE AND UTILITY
High performance combined with limited utility marks the specials and show cars, most of them one-offs. This category is hardly of significance when contemplating the purchase of such a car. Merely *finding* one is the greatest hurdle. Rumors that various show cars have been carefully hidden away at Lansing or the design center should not be believed. Sadly, most were destroyed, and I list descriptions without too much hope.

PROBLEM AREAS
As with all one-off cars, replacement hardware simply does not exist. So anything missing—which can be documented through the Oldsmobile Club of America and factory photographs—will have to be faricated. On the other hand, fiberglass construction of certain early models renders bodywork relatively easy.

SUMMARY AND PROSPECTS
Unlimited appreciation potential, but already they are very expensive. (When a Chrysler one-off—the Adventurer II—surfaced recently in New England, it carried an asking price of $250,000. And it needed work!)

PRODUCTION
Almost invariably, one of each.

The 1959 F-88 Mark II carried along the original F-88's two-seater design notions with contemporary ideas, though it was much cleaner than production '58 Olds models. Concave wheel arches will be familiar to Corvette folk; Olds had actually abandoned the oval bumper-grille by the time this special was seen.

Harley Earl took the F-88 Mark III with him and drove it personally after his retirement. Retractable roof shows that GM was interested in the contemporary production Ford Skyliner; the latter's failure to sell probably convinced them not to make one of their own. Top-down, the Mark III was only 46 inches high.

The Firefrost silver X215 was a modified convertible with Jetfire power under the hood. Fiberglass tonneau with built-in airfoil covered the rear seats, which was a clever touch.

Another Olds special seen at Chicago in 1963 was El Torero, a stock 98 convertible finished in Firefrost gold with a special brocaded interior.

Custom 4-4-2 from 1965, mildly modified from stock, with special grille and wheel covers.

Chicago Auto Show J-TR carried along the
X215 themes in 1963, again with Jetfire power
under the hood.

Appendix

The Oldsmobile Club of America
1897-1987

★★★★★

HISTORY

The Oldsmobile Club of America was founded in 1970 and covers all the cars listed in this book. More than 4,000 members worldwide and headquartered in Oldsmobile's hometown of Lansing, Michigan.

PERFORMANCE AND UTILITY

Membership is highly useful for any owner of a collectible Oldsmobile. Members are entitled to a free ad in each issue of the club magazine, *Journey With Olds*; an annual national meet attracts up to 500 cars and thousands of visitors; and regional and chapter events are conducted widely. Chapters devoted to special models like the Hurst/

Olds or Rallye 350 provide important expertise to owners of such cars.

PROBLEM AREAS

One of the most successful one-make clubs in the world.

SUMMARY AND PROSPECTS

An indispensable adjunct to your Olds-collecting hobby, with strong prospects for future appreciation.

ADDRESS

Oldsmobile Club of America, PO Box 16216, Lansing, MI 48901.